KIDS Superbrands

YOUR GUIDE TO SOME OF THE BEST KIDS BRANDS IN BRITAIN 2006

Argentina Australia Austria Bulgaria Brazil Canada China Croatia
Czech Republic Denmark Ecuador Egypt Estonia Finland France
Germany Greece Hong Kong Hungary Iceland India Indonesia
Ireland Italy Japan Kuwait Latvia Lebanon Lithuania Malaysia
Mexico Morocco The Netherlands Norway Pakistan Philippines
Poland Portugal Romania Russia Saudi Arabia Serbia Singapore
Slovakia Slovenia South Africa South Korea Spain Sri Lanka
Sweden Switzerland Taiwan Thailand Turkey United Arab Emirates
United Kingdom United States of America

Brand Liaison Directors
Claire Pollock
Liz Silvester

Managing Editor
Angela Cooper

Editor
Elen Lewis

Design Co-Ordinator
Laura Hill

Designer
Chris Harris

Junior Account Executive
Christy Lyons

Special Thanks to:
Louis Breyer
Lucas Bywater
Fergus Parkinson
Max Parkinson
Francesca Pollock
Georgia Pollock
Matthew Pollock
Jacob Selwyn
Rufus Shotter

Other publications from Superbrands in the UK:
Superbrands Volume VII ISBN: 0-9547510-8-6
Business Superbrands Volume IV ISBN: 0-9547510-6-X
CoolBrands Volume IV ISBN: 0-9550824-1-2
Sport BrandLeaders Volume I ISBN: 0-9547510-4-3
eSuperbrands Volume II ISBN: 1-905652-00-3

For more information, or to order these books, email
brands@superbrands.org or call 01825 873133.

For Superbrands international publications email
brands@superbrands.org or call 0207 379 8884.

© 2006 Superbrands Ltd

Published by Superbrands Ltd
19 Garrick Street
London
WC2E 9AX

www.superbrands.org/uk

Printed in China

ISBN: 1-905652-01-1

John Noble
Director
British Brands Group

 The first thing to strike you from the case studies here is the age of the brands featured. Some are kids themselves while others have plenty of grey hairs, but have succeeded nevertheless in maintaining their relevance to today's youngest users. There is also a wide diversity of sectors represented, including publishing, entertainment and financial services.

These case studies are testament to the versatility and relevance of branding. Here are companies of all sizes, focused on delivering outstanding performance and value to the very particular requirements of parents and their children. They set themselves apart, innovating and investing to make sure they are the preferred choice.

The power of these brands hits home when you consider those that you grew up with, probably haven't experienced for many years, but which still evoke strong feelings of pleasure and attachment. These are lifelong feelings and the companies featured here should be applauded for creating those same precious feelings for today's generation of kids.

Paul Gostick
International Chairman
The Chartered Institute of Marketing

 Establishing a successful children's brand is a very challenging task as it calls for marketers to step outside of the 'grown-up' boundaries and analyse the market through the eyes of a different generation. It also carries with it substantial responsibility on the part of the professional marketer. Recently, the focus on the dietary and nutritional value of products targeted at children has brought such responsibility into sharp relief.

The high standards set by Kids Superbrands is a laudable initiative and Superbrands have selected a comprehensive range of powerful brands which showcase a diverse set of organisations and illustrates well the continual evolution and development in the children's market.

The Chartered Institute of Marketing encourages recognition of the positive contribution that professional and responsible marketing makes not only to the corporate bottom line, but also to the value creation process and society as a whole. These points are clearly demonstrated by the successful brands showcased in this issue of Kids Superbrands.

Tessa Gooding
Communications Director
IPA

 The IPA is delighted to endorse the latest book in the Superbrands series, which recognises brands that have been extraordinarily successful in their sector. Kids Superbrands highlights successful brands we are comfortably familiar with because we grew up with them – Haliborange, SMA, Sun-Pat and Tumble Tots. However, the following pages contain some surprises too – Speedo, Sainsbury's Kids and NIVEA Sun – which I would like to think shows a leaning towards a healthier lifestyle for our children. This book is not about advertising to children. It's about Kids Superbrands, which is something else altogether.

About
Kids Supebrands

This publication forms part of a pioneering and exciting programme that was founded with the aim of paying tribute to the UK's strongest kids brands.

A dedicated Kids Superbrands Council (listed below) has been formulated, consisting of eminent individuals who are well qualified to judge which are the nation's strongest kids brands. Each brand featured in this book has qualified to be featured based on the ranking of this council.

Through identifying these brands, and providing their case histories, the organisation hopes that people will gain a greater appreciation of the discipline of branding and a greater admiration for the brands themselves.

Kid Superbrands Council 2006

Molly Bedingfield
Executive Director
Global Angels Ltd

Dr Sanjay Chaudhuri MBBS Bsc
Co-founder
Tomorrow's Child

Barbie Clarke
Managing Director
Family Kids and Youth

Nick Davies
Managing Director
WWAV Rapp Collins Bristol

Elizabeth Day
Health and Parenting Specialist
Mothercare

Shari Donnenfeld
Senior Vice President,
Marketing and Communications
Jetix Europe Ltd

Ian Douthwaite
Managing Director
Dubit Ltd

Stuart Drexler
Executive Vice President,
Brand Development
Polly Pocket Group

Diane Earnshaw
Founder
Vox Pops International

Kirsten Grant
Marketing Director
Puffin Books

Jacqueline Harding
BBC Education Editor
Director, Tomorrow's Child

David Leigh
Associate Marketing Director
Mamas & Papas

Rob Mansfield
Senior Editor, Kids and Teens
AOL UK

Michele Norton
Managing Director
Norton & Company Marketing
Communications Ltd

Tim Patten
Marketing Director
The Chelsea Store Group

Emma Sherski
Marketing and Licensing Director
Vivid Imaginations

Karen Wint
Director of Fundraising
Tommy's, the baby charity

Donna Price
Chairperson
Kids Superbrands Council

Contents

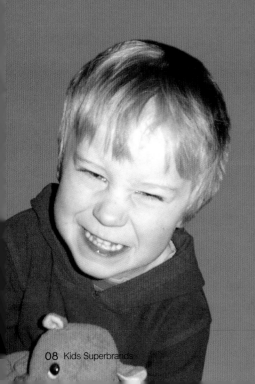

Foreword
Angela Cooper
Managing Editor

Having children is, without a doubt, a life changing experience which sparks a whole spectrum of emotions – from joy to fear. It also opens the door to another world that one may otherwise be completely unaware of.

During this odyssey, a wealth of both emotional and practical decisions await. Given that parents want to do the best they can for their child, brands in this arena have a special responsibility to meet the needs of this often bamboozled group of consumers.

In this first Kids Superbrands publication, we champion some of the strongest kids brands in Britain who offer advice and support as well as quality products and services to help pave the way along the journey of parenthood.

Additionally, we recognise the brands which are aimed at children and have taken on and succeeded in the challenge of communicating responsibility with a young audience.

At the back of this publication, some of the members of our independent and voluntary Kids Superbrands Council discuss key issues affecting children today. The topics discussed include the importance of reading, the power of play, trends in the children's market as well as the importance of responsible branding.

Finally, I hope that you find the cover of this publication suitably jam-resistant and the pages not too easy to be bitten or torn by your budding little branding experts....

Key

You will find the following symbols in the top right hand corner of each case study that indicate which age group the brand is for. The categories are;

Pregnancy   **Baby**   **Toddler**   **School Age**   **Whole family**

Child Development

From conception through to adolescence, the way in which a child develops is fascinating. Here is a snapshot of these amazing years.

By 12 weeks the unborn baby is already fully formed. The main organs are complete and all that is left is for the baby to continue to grow and develop. Finger and toe nails have begun to form and the baby measures about 7cm from head to bottom. At this very early stage the top of the uterus can usually be felt beginning to rise out of the pelvis.

An Australian study to examine whether raspberry leaf tea can ease labour found that those women who had taken raspberry leaf tablets had a substantially shorter second stage of labour and a lower rate of

forceps delivery (19.3% versus 30.4%). The study advised against raspberry leaves being used until the last two months of pregnancy due to their stimulating effect on the uterus. If used any earlier there is a risk of stimulating early labour.

Babies are born sociable and need an adult partner to develop their social skills. Playing involves being engaged in an enjoyable activity and if parents begin playing with their baby as soon as it is conceived, babies will become familiar with and recognise their parents' voices. Interaction can start from when the baby kicks and if gently tapped the bump may surprise prospective parents by responding.

The pale line (linea alba), that runs from the belly button to the top of the pubic bone, is skin coloured, so normally invisible in women. However, during pregnancy this line darkens to become a linea negra (Latin for black line). This darkening is caused by increases in estrogen and progesterone, which in turn step up production of the pigment melanin, a condition known as hyper-pigmentation. Inexplicably, the linea negra is far less prominent in fair skinned women, than in women with darker pigmentation.

From birth, babies have a working temperature control mechanism, like adults, which enables them to generate body warmth when they get cold. But unlike adults they can't conserve the warmth and become cold very quickly if the surrounding air is at a lower temperature than normal. This risk increases when they are undressed because babies have a relatively large surface area, compared to their body weight, which means they lose heat quickly. This may explain why historically, babies were always kept 'swaddled', even in warm conditions.

Breast milk is one of nature's super-foods. It contains just the right amount of fat, protein, carbohydrate, vitamin and minerals for babies and has the added bonus of being ready made and served at precisely the right temperature. Although it contains more fat than cow's milk it is easier for babies to absorb – this is one of the reasons why breastfed babies have different stools from bottle-fed babies; loose, with no smell and yellow or mustard in colour.

It's perfectly normal for babies of both sexes to have swollen breasts for the first three to five days after birth. These may even have a small quantity of 'milk' in them. This is due to hormones flooding through the mother just after birth – although the hormones are intended for her they sometimes transfer to the baby too.

Contrary to popular belief even one-day old babies do not spend all their time

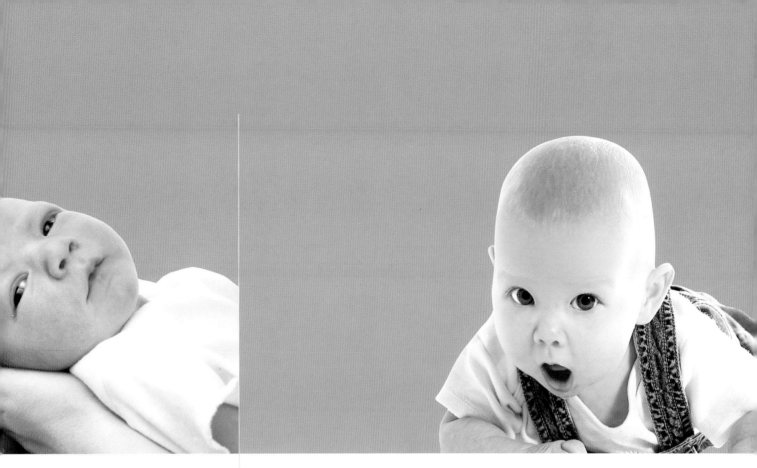

asleep or feeding. They can spend anything from one or two hours awake and are capable of becoming bored and craving for human company or something new to look at – a human face ranks highest on their wish list.

A newborn's head is very large in proportion to the rest of the body, and the cranium is enormous relative to his or her face. While the adult human skull is about an eighth of the total body length, the newborn's is twice that. At birth, many regions of the newborn's skull have not yet been converted to bone. These 'soft spots' are known as fontanelles.

Newborns are born wet, bloody, and coated in a white substance known as vernix caseosa, which is believed to act as an anti-bacterial barrier. The newborn may also have Mongolian spots, strawberry-style birthmarks or peeling skin, particularly at the wrists, hands, ankles, and feet. Immediately after birth, a newborn's skin is tinged grey or dusky blue in colour, but this becomes flesh coloured as soon as the baby begins to breathe.

While still inside the mother, a baby can hear many external noises including human voices, music and most other sounds. Therefore, a newborn can hear and relate to sound from birth. For inexplicable reasons they usually respond to a female's voice over a male's, which may explain why people unknowingly raise the pitch of their voice when talking to newborns.

Teething can start as early as three months or as late as 12 months. It will then take up to several years for all 20 'baby' or 'milk' teeth to grow. The teeth tend to emerge in pairs, and usually sooner in females than in males, although the exact patterns and onset of teething appears to be hereditary. When and how teeth appear in an infant has no bearing on the healthiness or developmental ability of the child.

According to the British Dental Association babies are less likely to suffer from prominent displaced teeth or misalignment of the jawline, in later life, if they suck dummies rather than sucking their thumbs. Many dentists also support the theory that dummies actually help to reduce tooth decay because they encourage the production of saliva.

Colic usually affects babies from around two weeks of age, peaks at about six weeks, and tails off after the third month. Some babies cry on and off for much of the day, but mostly colic hits in the evenings, between 6-12pm, with some babies continuing to cry inconsolably, long past any reasonably civilised bedtime.

By six months of age most babies can produce a whole range of playful sounds that enable them to experiment with different rhythms and volume. They become quite adept at this stage at using these sound-making skills to conduct simple conversational exchanges with adults or older children.

Babies' as young as a few months old can be fascinated by shiny pictures and often scrabble at the image, as if they are trying to get hold of the objects shown. This progresses until by about six or seven months, babies are able to enjoy being shown pictures in books – although they are likely to rip paper pages.

Babies' five senses are working from birth and within the limits set by their own physical abilities even very young babies are exploring and absorbing information; learning within the early months the boundaries between their own body and the rest of the world. Babies can also learn the effects of their own actions, like when they bite their own toes or inadvertently hit themselves with a rattle.

It is around the time of its first birthday that a child's memory emerges. This is the age that toddlers begin to remember things from the past and to anticipate familiar situations. From 12-18 months of age toddlers are usually able to recall another person's action and repeat it later on, enabling them to learn from what they see around them.

While a toddler may remember people, places, songs and smells as well as adults do its memory for some kinds of details is still very short. As a baby this was neither important nor very obvious but as a toddler

trying to do more grown up things, it is both vital and conspicuous. For example, much to their frustration, they will trip over a step between the kitchen and living room many times until repeated experience etches it into their memory.

When babies become toddlers, negative emotions that can manifest as behaviour problems, like tantrums. These are commonly referred to as 'the terrible twos'. Children are beginning to recognise and share their feelings and learning how to make their own decisions, express their needs and gain independence from their parents. All of which can be very frustrating and lead to boredom and anger, emotions that are as much a part of growing up as curiosity and discovery.

Most toddlers can't jump. This is all to do with physics. At birth, babies' arms and legs are far smaller, in proportion to the rest of their bodies, than their heads. Smaller limbs mean shorter, smaller muscles, so young children have much less muscle mass in their legs than adults do, in comparison with the rest of their bodies.

Hence, with their short, chubby legs, and weak muscles, most toddlers do not have enough strength to launch their big-headed bodies off the ground.

In the 12 months from the age of two to three years, children have a rapidly expanding vocabulary of around a few hundred words. Most children of this age are able to put sets of these words together to form short sentences and begin to ask simple questions.

Young children (3-4 year-olds) love to apply their physical skills to everyday activities that adults may dismiss as dull and tedious. For example, children of this age enjoy becoming involved in domestic tasks such as cooking, washing up and tidying. From the child's point of view washing up offers two things; the enjoyment of messing about with water and bubbles and a chance to act like a grown-up.

Three and four year-olds are often fascinated by watches and other time pieces – this is possibly linked to their growing awareness of numbers. They start to gauge some understanding of different times of the day since they can link ideas of time and time passing to routines and some of their usual daily activities.

Between the ages of three and five children become very interested in other people – how they behave and what they look like. They start to become aware of the differences between the sexes and outward signs of differing ethnic or cultural identities. Their view of these differences is not necessarily positive or negative, rather it can just be solely descriptive.

Children as young as five year-olds have a view of themselves, a sense of self-worth or level of self-esteem in which there is a balance of positives and negatives. Their resulting behaviour, including what they say, will be a reflection of this view. They are at an age where they have reached conclusions about themselves as to whether they are 'basically ok' – although this can change over time.

From the age of five children become more knowledgeable about animal and plant-life and the conditions that they need to flourish, often showing signs of being aware of and concerned about their local environment. From being able to recognise and describe changes in the weather, six and seven year-olds may, in addition, ask detailed questions about what causes rainbows or thunder and lightening.

At around six years of age boy's masculinity becomes 'switched on'. Suddenly they want to wear Superman capes, play with swords, fight, wrestle and generally make lots of noise. It is also around this time that boys 'lock on' to their father or male role model and want to learn from him and copy him – effectively they want to study how to be male.

Boys and girls feel pain differently and these gender differences start young, according to a recent Canadian study in which boys rated having teeth braces tightened as being more painful than girls did. Girls, on the other hand, typically reported that a broken arm hurt them more than it did boys. Emotional reaction to pain between the genders is also different; it makes girls fearful and anxious whereas it makes boys angry.

The speed at which children's bones heal is quite remarkable. Adults with a bone injury can expect to be in plaster for anything from six weeks to three months. Most children, however, have full use of their limbs within four weeks, because their bones are still growing, and the younger the child, the faster the recovery.

Despite popular conceptions, children are not always more flexible than adults and girls are not always as flexible as boys. Decreases in flexibility occur throughout childhood and adolescence as a direct result of growth. As the bones grow, the junction of the muscle and the tendon tightens across the joint. This loss of flexibility makes the young adolescent vulnerable to injury from a jarring action such as jumping or kicking or from long-term over-use.

The age at which puberty begins has dropped significantly since the 1840s, from about 17 years of age to 12 – although this varies from child-to-child.

When a child is ready to begin puberty, their pituitary gland (a pea-shaped gland located at the bottom of their brain) releases special hormones that go to work on different parts of the body, causing major physical and emotional changes to occur. It is universally accepted that puberty marks a child's transition into adulthood.

Kids Superbrands 2006 Council Members

Molly Bedingfield

Dr Sanjay Chaudhuri
Then and now

Barbie Clark
Barbie with her boys
Woody (1) and Stanley (3)

Nick Davies
Nick and Jo with their boys
Alby (2) and Jake (5)

Elizabeth Day
Liz with her children
Rebecca (9) and Alex (12)

Shari Donnenfeld
Then and now

Ian Douthwaite
Then and now

Stuart Drexler
Then and now

Diane Earnshaw
Diane and John with their
children Stephanie, Jenna
and Dan (left to right)

Molly Bedingfield
Executive Director
Global Angels Ltd
www.globalangels.org
Molly Bedingfield understands how brands interact with young people, with 20 years experience in the education sector and supporting children's charities.

Molly has professional experience as a counsellor and physiotherapist; as a head teacher of two schools; and as a home educator to her four children, including international music artists Daniel Bedingfield and Natasha Bedingfield.

As founder of the international children's charity, Global Angels, Molly is realising her life's passion to spark a revolution in kindness by supporting grass-roots children's projects worldwide.

Dr Sanjay Chaudhuri
MBBS Bsc
Co-founder, Tomorrow's Child
www.tomorrowschild.co.uk
Dr Sanjay Chaudhuri is a Co-founder of Tomorrow's Child, an organisation devoted to the welfare of children of the digital age. He is passionate about children's welfare and has written for CBeebies online, regarding nutrition and was recently appointed as a researcher for Creative Partnerships, looking into the scientific nature of creativity. Sanjay is also a speaker on the fascinating link between creativity, emotions and health. He is currently writing a book concerning the digital nature of humanity and exploring creative intelligence in children.

Sanjay qualified as a medical doctor from Guy's Hospital and also has a research degree in Radiological Imaging. His years of research in the field of psychology, medicine, science, and biofeedback, have led him to establish a link between creativity and health, and between digital electronics and the bio-electronic body.

Sanjay continues to practice preventative health medicine in Hampshire and Harley Street, mostly to senior executives from the business community.

Barbie Clarke
Managing Director
Family Kids and Youth
www.kidsandyouth.com
Barbie runs Family Kids and Youth, a company she set up with a small team of researchers four years ago. She is also Editor of Young Consumers. A youth researcher for 20 years, Barbie works closely with Family Kids and Youth clients on research and consultancy dealing with children and young people's issues. Previously she ran the Family division of NOP (National Opinion Poll).

Barbie has a post-graduate qualification in psycho-analytical counselling and worked for several years in a therapeutic setting in a men's prison, and in a secondary school. She currently counsels teenagers each week in Tower Hamlets, London.

An accomplished and experienced speaker, Barbie regularly gives papers at international conferences, writes articles, and appears on TV and radio commenting on youth research. She works with several well known food manufacturers and retailers, and has written extensively on the issues around children's lifestyle and diet. Barbie is on the BBC Children's Editorial Board.

Nick Davies
Managing Director
WWAV Rapp Collins Bristol
www.wwavrcbristol.co.uk
Nick is Managing Director of WWAV Rapp Collins Bristol, part of the global Rapp Collins direct marketing agency network. Nick has worked for direct marketing agencies for 16 years on a wide variety of financial, charity and FMCG brands. Many of these have involved specific activity to younger audiences, such as projects for Microsoft and Tesco Kids Club.

WWAV presently works with numerous children's organisations, including NSPCC, UNICEF and The Children's Society. Nick is currently working on a research project with Bath University to develop a better understanding of how brands should market responsibly with regards children.

Nick is a Council Member of the DMA West and IDM West. He lives near Bath with his wife and two sons.

Elizabeth Day
Health and Parenting Specialist
Mothercare
www.mothercare.com
Elizabeth has worked for Mothercare as a health and parenting expert since 1990. She previously worked in a variety of educational and childcare roles, gaining a wealth of experience relating to babies, children and parenting.

It is of paramount importance to Mothercare that it turns its understanding of parent's aspirations, wants and needs into the design of excellent, useable and affordable products.

Mothercare was founded in 1961 and is still the leading parent and baby care retailer in its domestic market. They have 240 stores across the UK, a thriving catalogue and website business, as well as 262 stores internationally in 36 countries that focus on helping parents and their children.

Mothercare is also very proud of its award in 2005 as one of 'The Sunday Times 10 Best Big Companies to Work for' (as voted for by Mothercare employees). Mothercare employs more than 5,200 people.

Shari Donnenfeld
Senior Vice President,
Marketing and Communications
Jetix Europe Ltd
www.jetixeurope.com
In her current role, Shari is responsible for directing the brand strategy and communications, and providing consumer insights for all Jetix businesses. Operationally, Shari oversees the pan-European Marketing, Production, Research and Press and PR teams, each of which supervises all local and pan-European activity.

Shari joined Jetix Europe as Executive Director of Research and Marketing, in September 2000. Prior to this, she was based at Nickelodeon as Director of Research and Planning. Previously, she worked as an account manager at the advertising agency FCB/Leber Katz Partners, on the Nabisco and Colgate Palmolive accounts. Shari's past experience also includes teaching at primary and high school levels.

Ian Douthwaite
Managing Director
Dubit Ltd
www.dubit.co.uk
Ian is one of the founders and Managing Director of Dubit Limited, a business he helped a group of teenagers set up in 1999. Dubit, a youth research and communications company, was the natural corollary of Ian's extensive work with young people. From Dubit's initial aims of making research and marketing companies listen more closely to what young people want and involving kids at the heart of the business, the company now boasts 400,000 young members across the UK.

Ian began this youth work fulltime after graduating in Economics and growing and selling a successful business in 1993. He invested more time in developing projects with teenagers, in Scouts and other Youth Groups through Duke of Edinburgh Awards, Young Enterprise and helping with youth homelessness in and around Leeds. This experience led through to supporting the principle of Dubit, in getting kids involved in youth marketing and developing better products through their involvement.

Stuart Drexler
Executive Vice President,
Brand Development
Polly Pocket Group
www.PollyPocket.co.uk
Stuart oversees brand development for Polly Pocket, the world's number one small doll for the last five years (Source: The NPD Group, Inc.). Responsible for growing Polly Pocket into a lifestyle brand, Stuart bridges toy, entertainment and licensing efforts to drive innovation throughout the business with a consumer-centric approach.

With over 15 years experience directing kids and youth brands, Stuart has created award-winning toys, stories and interactive media for many key kids' brands including Elmo, Action Man, Barbie and LEGO. At LEGO, Stuart led product development to originate the Knights Kingdom franchise, named 2005 Toy Of The Year for boys.

Stuart first honed his brand skills at Ogilvy & Mather advertising following his training in Social Sciences from the University of California at Berkeley. Further qualifications include a Master of Technology in Education degree from Harvard. Stuart prides himself on generating quality mass media content, which is enjoyed by kids and valued by parents.

Diane Earnshaw
Founder
Vox Pops International
www.voxpops.co.uk
Diane started her career in advertising before moving on to work for Mintel. She went on to found Vox Pops International, the pioneers of video based research, using video to conduct and deliver qualitative research. Since the company was established in 1987 they have produced more than 3,000 research videos for over 500 clients internationally.

Diane's experience in researching youth and kids goes back to 1997 when she established Youthscene – an international video study, with over 800 youngsters from Europe and the USA. During the last four years Diane has managed studies with more than 500 face to face video interviews, with children throughout the UK on issues relating to healthy eating, leisure, technology, media, social issues such as bullying, marketing and advertising.

In addition to regularly conducting research with children she is also a mother of three, all pre-teens. Her real achievement in life at present is trying to balance their needs with a hectic work schedule!

Kids Superbrands 2006 Council Members

Kirsten Grant
Kirsten with her niece
Freya (3)

Jacqueline Harding

David Leigh
David and Caroline
with their daughter
Holly Rose (1)

Rob Mansfield
Rob with his daughter
Beth (2)

Michele Norton
Michele with her twin
girls (6) Anabelle (left)
and Charlotte

Tim Patten
Then and now

Emma Sherski
Then and now

Karen Wint
Then and now

Donna Price
Then and now

Kirsten Grant
Marketing Director
Puffin Books
www.puffin.co.uk
Kirsten has spent 10 extremely eventful years at Puffin Books, working in various roles, to finally becoming Marketing Director in 2005.

Since starting at Puffin, Kirsten has witnessed an evolution of children's publishing, moving from a small, cosy world to one of the big players in marketing terms, with bigger bestsellers, bigger expectations and bigger marketing budgets to help achieve real stand-out in the marketplace. A huge part of the role Kirsten relishes is the challenge of launching bestselling brands into the marketplace, such as Eoin Colfer's Artemis Fowl, Young Bond, Angelina Ballerina and Roald Dahl.

Jacqueline Harding
BBC Education Editor
Director, Tomorrow's Child
www.tomorrowschild.co.uk
Jacqueline is passionate about making life simply amazing for children. She has an eye on their future needs and her work as BBC Education Editor, Director of 'Tomorrow's Child', and internationally recognised Author for adults and children, testifies to her professional commitment to raising the bar.

Exuberance and effervescence ensures she seizes every opportunity within the media to make learning fun for children. Everyday life finds her consulting on children's TV, advising on the Development of DVDs (such as Teletubbies), writing CBeebies online, creating 'Lets all make music with the Tweenies,' and speaking on radio.

And, as a previous headteacher and DfES consultant, it makes sense for her to be working tirelessly to promote the needs of children. Ms Jacqueline Harding MA, CERT.ED; completed a PhD in the effects of the media on young children and has since gained special recognition with The Fab award for Best Ambassador for BBC Worldwide, April 2004.

David Leigh
Associate Marketing Director
Mamas & Papas
www.mamasandpapas.com
David has worked in marketing for the last 10 years. Learning his trade at ASDA in the late 1990s, which was bought by Wal-Mart in 2001, when they entered the UK market.

Delivering in all aspects of marketing, from brand management through to category management and new product launches, David worked in the FMCG arena, joining Mamas & Papas in early 2004.

One of the attractions of Mamas & Papas for David was the different and challenging skill set required by marketers in this area. With only circa 650,000 births a year and limited channels of effective distribution, David has found this role to be a real creative challenge.

Since David joined Mamas & Papas, the marketing department has gone from strength to strength. The business has increased its routes to market and is now available through mail order and online with sales ensuring that Mamas & Papas is the number one brand in the market (Source: FSA).

Rob Mansfield
Senior Editor, Kids and Teens
AOL UK
www.aol.co.uk
Rob joined AOL in November 2004, bringing more than 10 years experience in youth magazines to his online role.

As Senior Editor, he oversees the content on AOL's popular Kids and Teens channels, which includes music, movies, chat, homework help, games, and advice. He has recently been involved in the launch of two new online areas for younger AOL Broadband members called Zoo and X.

Prior to AOL, Rob worked on a variety of youth titles including Young Telegraph, Looks, Disney's Big Time, Mizz, Bliss and More. He has also written for magazines such as Glamour, Marie Claire and the Radio Times and worked at the BBC, Emap, Express Newspapers and Trinity Mirror.

In his spare time, Rob enjoys doing Bob the Builder puzzles with his two year-old daughter Beth, pictured, and is looking forward to the birth of a new baby in the Spring.

Michele Norton
Norton & Company Marketing Communications Ltd
Managing Director
www.nortonandcompany.com
Michele has worked in PR for over 20 years on some of the best known children's brands crossing sectors as diverse as toys, baby food, nappies, retail, publishing, confectionery, grocery and more. Michele set up Norton & Company Marketing Communications Ltd, 15 years ago, to specialise primarily in the PR and marketing of children's and youth brands. Over this time her clients have included Vivid Imaginations, LEGO, Mattel, Warner Bros., VTech, Corgi and JCB. She has worked with many new and evergreen brands such as Bratz, Thunderbirds, Barbie, Crayola, Spiderman, Thomas the Tank Engine, Sega and Silver Cross.

Michele is married with twin six year old girls and lives in Oxfordshire.

Tim Patten
Marketing Director
The Chelsea Store Group
www.elc.co.uk
Tim joined Chelsea Stores Holdings Ltd in 2004, as part of the management team involved in the buyout of Early Learning Centre. Prior to this, he had an extensive career in advertising and direct marketing, working for Abbott Mead Vickers and latterly as Managing Partner of Proximity London. He was also the Founding Partner and Managing Director of Harrison Patten Troughton Brand Response, and a former Head of Communications for BT. Tim is married with a five year-old son and a four year-old daughter, who both think their father has the best job in the world.

Emma Sherski
Marketing and Licensing Director
Vivid Imaginations
www.evivid.co.uk
Emma graduated from the University of the West of England, Bristol in 1994 with a degree in Psychology and went on to complete a post graduate diploma and Masters in Marketing at Kingston University, publishing a paper on 'Consumer Confusion over Copycat branding'.

In 1995 Emma started her career working for Japanese toy company Tomy and enjoyed a secondment to Tokyo during her five year career working on product development and marketing of the core, pre-school Tomy brand.

In 2001 Emma moved on to become Marketing Director for an Independent Production Company working on ITV and BBC children's programming and International Licensing.

Emma joined British Toy Company Vivid Imaginations in 2003 as Marketing and Licensing Director across the total toy and gift portfolio. Over this period, market share has grown to 8.6% (Source: NPD J-D 2005) propelling Vivid into becoming the second largest toy company with brands such as Bratz, Thunderbirds, Disney, Balamory and the annoying thing Crazy Frog, contributing to the companies most recent success.

Karen Wint
Director of Fundraising
Tommy's, the baby charity
www.tommys.org
After gaining a marketing degree Karen began her career marketing fragrances with Avon. Since then she has worked for high profile charities; NCH, Comic Relief and Cystic Fibrosis Trust before joining Tommy's in 1999. Karen has taken Tommy's fundraising team from being inexperienced and enthusiastic to one of the most professional and progressive organisations in the sector. Income has risen by 75%, and fundraising cost/income ratio has improved consistently. Karen has earned the respect of many leading and trusted organisations in the baby and children's sectors by devising partnerships, which deliver real value to their brands. At the root of it all is Karen's desire to make a difference to the lives of many families in the UK by making pregnancy and childbirth safer for all. Karen applies the same energy and dedication to everything she does; being a keen Salsa dancer, a film fanatic, enjoying the arts and all round good health guru as well as keeping her husband Warren, her family and many friends in order.

Donna Price
Chairperson
Kids Superbrands Council
Donna joined Superbrands as Commercial Director in April 2005. At Superbrands Donna heads up the UK operation and is responsible for the marketing, PR, editorial and sales process for all of the UK programmes. She also chairs three other Superbrands Councils including, Kids Superbrands, Superbrands and CoolBrands.

Previously, Donna spent three years at The Mirror Group where she was responsible for the launch of both M magazine and M Celebs. Both of these launches represented a significant strategic move to take The Mirror slightly more upmarket.

Prior to this Donna worked at Emap for nine years, where she worked on some of the UK's premiere magazine brands including Elle, FHM, Sky, Mixmag and Kerrang!

Her experience spans a mixture of advertising, marketing and publishing.

adams kids is a specialist fashion retailer for kids aged 0-10 years-old. The brand purely focuses on childrenswear and holds a differentiated position on the high street. adams kids can be found in over 300 shops in the UK and 112 stores internationally.

What is adams kids?

adams kids is a children's clothing specialist. It has been selling kids fashion on the high street for over 70 years in the UK. The brand's range provides kids clothing and accessories for each of the child's life stages.

These include the 'Little Bundle' collection created especially for babies from 0-12 months, which features soft touch fabrics and easy fastenings.

For toddlers, there are collections for both girls and boys aged nine months to four years-old. The collections include denim, trendy tops, sportswear and smart outfits and characters such as Thomas the Tank Engine and Dora the Explorer. All the collections are easy-to-wear and designed to stand up to the rough and tumble of toddlers.

For boys and girls aged 3-10 years there is denim, sportswear and character ranges from Barbie to Batman. For school time, there is a range of practical but trendy schoolwear available throughout the year. adams kids schoolwear features adjustable waists and longer length on all woven trousers to cater for growing kids.

In addition to this, for the special events in a child's life, such as being a bridesmaid or pageboy, adams kids has a range of occasionwear for kids from 2-10 years.

Where would you have seen the brand?

As a retail brand, adams kids is always visible on the high street. It has over 300 shops in towns, city centres and shopping malls across the UK. It also has over 100 stores overseas. adams kids is a popular brand in the Middle East with stores in countries such as Saudi Arabia, United Arab Emirates and Kuwait. It also has stores in many European destinations including Slovakia, Malta and Greece.

Over the last 18 months, adams kids has also diversified by forming a series of business partnerships. This means that in addition to its solo shops, it has concessions in various department stores, and supplies Sainsbury's for its TU kidswear range and Boots for its mini mode range. The adams childrenswear group of companies now trades from over 1,000 UK outlets.

The adams kids website also plays a crucial role in marketing and developing the retail brand. Customers can browse the fashion collections online, find out what is going on in their local store, get advice on everything from fashion trends to health and safety for kids and also buy clothes at www.adamkids.co.uk.

adams kids has also won a number of awards which have boosted its profile. In March 2004, the brand was presented with an award to recognise its 10-year association with its corporate charity, Save the Children, which it has raised over £2 million for.

adams kids now supports WellChild as its corporate charity, through both

fundraising and supporting local events, such as the company directors helping to create a multi-sensory garden at a disabled boy's home in Birmingham.

In 2002, adams kids' schoolwear was celebrated by Woman's Own magazine, passing its Tried and Tested survey. Readers of Best magazine also voted adams kids the Best Children's Fashion Retailer in 2002.

What does the brand promise you?

adams kids is a retail brand that focuses on delivering what parents and kids need and want. As one of the only specialist kids fashion retailers on the high street, the brand can offer value for money, personal service, with informative and knowledgeable staff on hand at all times, and a child-friendly environment. In short, an enjoyable, hassle-free shopping experience.

How was the brand developed?

adams kids was established in 1933, when Amy Adams set up a child's clothing business from her terraced house in Kings Heath, Birmingham. For 40 years the company operated as an independent retailer until it was bought by the Foster Brothers in 1973. In the first two years of their partnership the brand, then known as adams opened 30 more shops.

During the early 1980s, adams grew to over 215 stores across the country; until 1985 when Foster Bothers was acquired by Sears. By the 1990s adams had become an important brand in the kidswear market.

In 1993, the retail brand chose to support Save the Children as its corporate charity, beginning a long partnership. In 1997, adams first international franchise opened in Saudi Arabia. Another key landmark came in 1999, when following a management buy out, adams became a privately owned company. In the same year, the brand opened its first Sainsbury's/Savacentre concession.

The brand teamed up with Boots in 2002 to launch a childrenswear range called 'mini mode' and opened new stores in India and Greece.

In 2003, as adams celebrated its 70th birthday, it joined other retailers including Sainsbury's, Debenhams and BP to offer its customers the Nectar reward scheme. The following year adams launched a new range of clothing in Sainsbury's called the TU collection.

In 2005, following the appointment of a new chief executive Dean Murray, the retailer re-branded to adams kids and introduced a new logo and brand identity, which is currently being rolled out. It is hoped that the re-brand will see adams kids become the best specialist children's fashion clothing store on the high street.

The brand has launched three new concept stores in Leamington Spa, Leeds White Rose and Meadowhall. The new stores were designed to make shopping for kids' clothes more fun and inviting. They include boys and girls changing rooms, a spacious footwear section, bright in-store graphics and kids' play activities – including interactive games and mini shopping trolleys.

Did you know?

469,000 pairs of grey school trousers are sold in one year.

The adams kids lorries travel 780,000 miles a year which equates to 15,000 miles a week.

Over five million babies have been born in the UK since adams began in 1933.

adams kids have been selling fashion for three generations.

bambino mio ®

As consumers become increasingly aware of their social responsibility to the world around them, Bambino Mio's range of natural, environmentally-friendly nappies and covers tap into a burgeoning trend. The reusable nappies are made from 100% cotton and offer many advantages over disposable alternatives.

Cotton is natural so it allows baby's skin to breathe, helping to maintain a healthy temperature. It is also soft and naturally absorbent so there's no need for gels or chemicals near baby's delicate skin to increase absorbency. Also, as cotton nappies are reusable they offer substantial savings to parents compared with disposables.

What is Bambino Mio?

Bambino Mio provides a complete 'nappy system' suitable for babies from newborn to potty training stage (around two and a half years) featuring 100% cotton nappies, waterproof nappy covers and biodegradable nappy liners.

The product range also includes Swim Nappies, Training Pants, a Nappy Bucket, Laundry Bags, Muslin Squares and a stylish Baby Change Rucksack. It also offers a range of environmentally responsible nappy care products including Mio Liners, Mio Care washing powder and Mio Fresh biodegradable nappy cleanser, all of which can be used with other reusable nappy brands.

Bambino Mio long-lasting nappies offer maximum absorbency and can be folded in various ways to suit a baby's needs. They are made with tightly woven, high quality, cotton.

For consumer convenience Bambino Mio also supplies three different economical sets for parents. Nappy Sets, a starter pack featuring 12 nappies and three covers; Birth to Potty Packs, which includes all the nappies and covers a baby will need from birth through to potty training stage; and an Accessories Pack, which complements the Birth to Potty pack with items to wash and care for babies and their nappies.

In the UK alone cotton nappy usage has grown in the last five years from 2% to 15%.

Bambino Mio distribute products to 50 countries around the world and this is set to increase as the company identifies opportunities for international expansion.

Where would you have seen the brand?

Bambino Mio products are sold through nursery stores, department stores, chemists, supermarkets and larger high street stores. In the UK and Republic of Ireland the brand is available in independent nursery stores and selected stores of John Lewis, Babies R Us, Daisy & Tom, Mothercare, Superquinn, Roches Stores, Morrisons, Lloyds Pharmacy, Unichem and Boots, to name a few.

The most high profile and effective marketing of the brand comes from the consumers themselves as Bambino Mio products consistently win consumer awards and are regularly featured in the UK's leading parenting magazines.

Bambino Mio has, to date, won 16 consumer press awards including winning the Mother & Baby Gold Award for Best Environmentally Friendly product in both 2001 and 2005. It also won, for the third successive year, the Prima Baby Reader Awards in 2005 for the best buy in the real nappy category.

The brand is also supported by a coherent marketing programme which combines national press advertising in key parental titles such as Mother & Baby, Pregnancy & Birth, Practical Parenting and Prima Baby, alongside consumer PR and promotions.

As part of its future growth plans Bambino Mio will continue to invest in brand building initiatives including media, PR, expanded retail distribution in both UK and international markets and attendance at leading consumer shows. Support from healthcare professions including midwives, who see the benefits of reusable nappies, is also a key element of the marketing programme.

How was the brand developed?

Husband and wife team, Guy and Jo Schanschieff founded the brand in 1997, following four years experience in the nappy laundering service market. Bambino Mio was initially set up as a mail order company selling reusable cotton nappies direct to consumers.

Realising the potential of reusable nappies, the Schanschieffs ran an advertising campaign in parenting magazines to build brand awareness. From that platform they started selling Bambino Mio products to independent baby shops.

After strengthening the sales department with a national account manager, Bambino Mio successfully secured product listings with major high street retailers and the brand is now stocked by a wide variety of high street stores.

As parents of three children, the Schanschieffs have continued to improve and expand the Bambino Mio range based on their first hand experiences and knowledge. Consumers, hospitals and nappy laundry services have all rigorously tested Bambino Mio products and constant improvements are made following feedback from customers.

The company now employs 19 dedicated staff at its headquarters in Brixworth, Northamptonshire as well as 25 exclusive international distributors to represent the brand across 50 markets supported by a multi-lingual website. In addition, it was named Northamptonshire Entrepreneurial Business of the Year in 2004.

What does the brand promise you?

In spite of strong growth, Bambino Mio remains true to the core brand values upon which the company was founded – to offer quality products that provide comfort and performance for baby as well as offering convenience, style and value for money for parents.

Bambino Mio strives to bring consumers the latest in innovation. Its on-going brand commitment is to design and develop products that surpass parents' expectations.

Bambino Mio is a natural, environmentally responsible product that is better for baby, convenient to use and exceptional value for money. The brand delivers a superior customer service and product experience, enabling parents to focus on the joys of parenthood.

Did you know?

The company name Bambino Mio was inspired by the 1994 TV film of the same name directed by Edward Bennett and featuring Julie Walters.

An estimated 4.2% of all babies in the UK are wearing Bambino Mio brand of re-usable cotton nappies.

Bambino Mio market share within the UK reusable nappies sector is estimated to be 30-35%.

Over one million Bambino Mio cotton nappies have been sold over the past two years.

Bambino Mio was awarded the prestigious Mother & Baby magazine Gold Award for Best Environmentally Friendly Product in 2001 and 2005 for the Nappy Set.

Bounty ®
...for growing families!

www.bounty.com

It's no accident that the dictionary refers to the word bounty as generosity or gift. Bounty is the UK's leading expert at marketing to young families, providing samples, free products and information to support them at key moments through pregnancy, birth and beyond. Its unique distribution and access to families through NHS hospitals, allows the brand to provide and support 96% of the UK birth rate through the famous Bounty packs. Major pharmaceutical companies and other leading brands work with Bounty to specifically reach families with young children.

What is Bounty?

During pregnancy and the early months after childbirth, women begin using products that they have little or no previous experience of, ranging from breast pads to folic acid and car seats. Bounty packs offer women an opportunity to sample and learn about some of these brands that are new to them.

It distributes timely information through three pre-natal packs including the Pregnancy Information, Mum-to-Be and Overnight Essentials packs and two post-natal packs including New Mum and Baby's Progress. Bounty packs include free information guides through pregnancy and birth until the child becomes a toddler, to add informative support for new families.

The Bounty guides are produced and updated by a panel of experts comprising

a breastfeeding expert, nutritionist, obstetrician and midwifery expert. The guides include 'Your Pregnancy', 'Your Baby', 'Weaning & Health' and 'Your Toddler'. Parents also receive a number of relevant and timely mailings from Bounty and its partners. This can include the Bounty guides, pack redemption claim cards, coupons and special offers.

As part of Bounty's hospital services, which distributes its packs to new mums, the brand also provides some hospitals with a photographic service. This offers

the opportunity to capture memories of a new family with high quality photos at the bedside.

The brand's consumer website www.bounty.com provides the largest online community forum specifically catering for young families. With around 400,000 registered users, the site offers advice and information on a range of parenting and family subjects as well as shopping, holidays, competitions and discussion forums.

Bounty also offers its consumers a number of products in other sectors such as financial services, for example, the Bounty Child Trust Fund. These are run in affiliation with leading service providers to ensure that young families receive the best deals and investments available on the market.

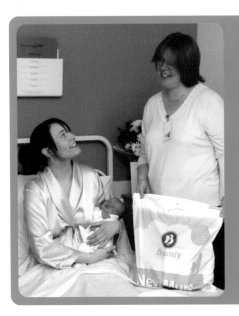

Where would you have seen the brand?

Unless you have experienced pregnancy or birth, you'll probably associate the name Bounty with coconut chocolate bars or kitchen towels. However, Bounty plays a vital role for new mums. In 2005 alone, it distributed over three million packs through its hospital and retail channels, Boots and Mothercare. Over the last half a century, Bounty has established itself as a key part of this life changing experience.

The first pack in the Bounty series, the Pregnancy Information pack, is issued by midwifes to expectant mothers at their initial appointment. Inside this pack is the 'Your Pregnancy' guide, containing a claim card to redeem a 'Mum-to-Be' pack from Boots or Mothercare. Once the expectant mum reaches the end of her pregnancy and is admitted to the hospital delivery suite, she is offered her 'Overnight Essentials' pack in preparation for her baby's birth.

Once mum has given birth, a 'Bounty lady' will hand her the 'New Mum' pack in the maternity ward before she is discharged. This flagship pack is distributed to approximately 96% of all new mums across the UK. When the child reaches 4-6 months of age, and is ready for weaning, the mother will be sent a claim card to redeem the Baby's Progress pack from one of Bounty's retail partners. The last Bounty guide in the series, Your Toddler, is sent to mums when their child nears their first birthday.

What does the brand promise you?

Families are at the heart of everything Bounty does. Its brand values are all about making family life easier. Over the last 47 years, Bounty has become established as a trustworthy, informative and empathetic provider for consumers. Bounty pledges to provide families with the information they need during pregnancy, birth and their child's first years. It also aims to provide a range of services to make choices about finance, learning and holidays as easy as possible.

How was the brand developed?

Bounty was founded in 1959 by Bill Hopewell-Smith with the launch of its first sample pack – The New Mother Pack. Six years later, Bounty launched their first information guide for families, 'Your Baby'.

In 1966, the Bounty Field Force was introduced to deliver its packs to new mums directly at the bedside. This pack became so popular that over the next few decades Bounty extended its portfolio and hundreds of brands got involved in the publications and sampling programmes.

The company launched with just six employees but has mushroomed to employ 550 people. Today Bounty distributes 3.2 million packs through a team of over 350 staff across NHS hospitals in the UK and their retail partners.

Over the past couple of years, Bounty has evolved from a mother and baby focused business towards a young family service provider with an extended portfolio and product offerings.

Did you know?

Bounty employs over 350 'Bounty ladies' to personally hand out the packs at the hospital bedside.

If you are under 40, it is likely that your mother received a Bounty pack when you were born.

Side by side, the Bounty New Mum packs distributed in 2005 would stretch from London to Leeds.

Alfa, Aston, Bentley, Ferrari, Ford, Kia, Lexus, Lotus, Mercedes, Morgan and Porsche are some of the less traditional baby names captured through the Bounty club.

Britax

Britax is an international brand recognisable for its emphasis on safety through its premium range of children's car seats and pushchairs. The brand has developed a reputation as an innovator. It is often the first brand to bring new technology and advances into the market. Britax Childcare covers pushchairs, car seats and bicycle seats – the whole area of safe travel for children. In the UK, Britax is a dominant player in the car seat sector, with 44% market share (Source: FSA).

What is Britax?

The Britax brand has traditionally been well-regarded for its emphasis on safety and technological expertise in the car seat market. Britax is the only manufacturer to produce in the UK and is proud to have the only UK product testing facilities at the head office in Andover. The brand has a wide product portfolio to cater for children from newborns to school age who are travelling in cars.

Car seats account for about 80% of Britax Childcare's total European sales, bicycle seats are a further 10%, and the remainder is what the company calls travel systems – pushchairs that you put a car seat onto.

More recently, the brand has increased its focus on style and comfort. This has seen Britax launching new fabrics and styling into its range to ensure it appeals to a wide cross section of consumers. It has also introduced the Comfi-Flex concept, which makes the Britax car seats more comfortable with softer fabrics and thicker wadding. This is based on extensive consumer research through its European research and development teams.

Britax's reputation as an innovator was sealed when it introduced ISOFIX into the children's car seat market in 1997. This is a method of fixing the car seat directly to the car without using a seat belt, eliminating the danger of fitting a seat incorrectly. This is a common problem among families as only 20% of conventional child seats are fitted correctly by parents and by comparison 96% of all ISOFIX seats are fitted correctly.

Last year, Britax launched a number of new products. They include a versatile children's car seat called Evolva 123, which has been designed to grow with its passenger and can carry a child from approximately nine months to 11 years-old. The Evolva 123 is designed to be used with its own harness from approximately nine months to four years-old and by a lap and diagonal belt from approximately 4-11 years-old.

The Evolva 123 was designed following European research and includes a number of different features. These include a multiple position, adjustable headrest – to cater for growing children – a recline position for longer journeys and curved sides to protect young passengers. It also includes a number of convenient features such as drink and snack holders. The Evolva 123 Ultra offers similar features as well as adjustable side wings and high levels of comfort.

This year, Britax launched a four-wheeled, flat-fold pushchair called the Voyaga, which is suitable for children from birth to four years-old. The product has large wheels with puncture-proof tyres as well as other features such as an adjustable height handle, spacious shopping basket, detachable hood and a full size PVC rain cover.

The Voyaga is also compatible with the Britax Cosy Tot Premium infant carrier, which can be used as a car seat and baby carrier. The carrier can be clicked onto the armrests of the Voyaga enabling parents to transfer babies easily from the car to the pushchair.

Where would you have seen the brand?

Britax's products are distributed through many channels including nursery shops, vehicle manufacturers, department stores, supermarkets, larger department stores and high street shops such as John Lewis, Mothercare, Babies 'R' Us and Halfords. The brand is also available through mail order and is promoted through exhibitions like the Baby&Child show.

Safety is a core brand value of Britax and plays a central role in its marketing campaigns. Tying in with the UK Government's focus on children's road safety, Britax linked up with Safeway and GMTV to run a daily TV campaign which offered advice to parents surrounding the issues of badly fitted car seats.

While the campaign was running, 10 regional 'checking stations' at Safeway stores enabled parents to glean advice from trained Britax experts. The brand also featured on the daily GMTV broadcasts which went out live at prime time.

What does the brand promise you?

The brand has one key aim which influences everything that it does – namely that Britax keeps people safe.

How was the brand developed?

Britax was established in the 1950s in the UK from an automotive background. It was launched out of the strong innovation environment of British Accessories and produced the first inertia seat belt. In 1997, it revolutionised the child car seat market with its launch of the ISOFIX system, a design which attaches the car seat to the vehicle without the use of a safety belt. At present ISOFIX seats require specific vehicle approval. As a result of direct crash tests, ISOFIX has now been approved for use in 130 vehicle models, with more on the way. The first and only car seat of this type on sale in the UK is the Duo ISOFIX, which has been available since 2002.

More recently, Britax has signed a global licensing agreement with Fisher Price to launch branded car seats. The Fisher Price range of car seats (with products from infant carriers through to booster seats) will offer the consumer safety and design, accompanied by the fun colourful styling associated with the Fisher Price brand.

Did you know?

The UK law is changing in September to say that kids must ride in children's car seats until they reach a minimum height of 1.35 metres and this will be enforced with on-the-spot fines.

Britax fitting checks have shown that more than 30% of child car seats are fitted incorrectly by parents, while another 31% needed minor adjustment.

Worldwide tests of ISOFIX seats found that 96% of parents fitted seats correctly.

BRITISH AIRWAYS
London eye

Towering above the city at 135 metres high, the British Airways London Eye is the world's largest observation wheel offering panoramic views across London and a unique perspective on some of the capital's most famous landmarks. The gradual flight in one of the 32 high-tech glass capsules takes approximately 30 minutes.

What is the British Airways London Eye?

The British Airways London Eye is a 21st century symbol for modern Britain that provides an inspiring experience with great views from a central location. The British Airways London Eye has tailored and selected its products and services to appeal to and involve all ages, ensuring that a wide range are child-friendly.

The London Eye River Cruise Experience offers a 40 minute sightseeing cruise on the Thames with live commentary presented by trained guides. The cruise takes in some of the major sites along the river with audio commentary also available in several foreign languages.

The London Eye has also developed deals with West End shows, leading London attractions such as Madame Tussaud's and London Zoo as well as child-friendly restaurants Pizza Express and The Rainforest Café to accompany the London Eye flight.

Additionally, the British Airways London Eye has created products which have an educational focus, to help children learn through their experience. For example, The Schools Discovery Flight delivered by a trained guide examines the River Thames and its role in London's development, which is relevant for the Key Stage 1 and 2 History and Geography curriculum. For teachers, the education section on the London Eye website (www.ba-londoneye.com) provides online resources for Key Stage 1 and 2.

Where would you have seen the brand?

The brand is promoted through campaigns that ensure that the right messages are communicated to the right people. Families are targeted through marketing in and around the key school holiday periods of Easter, summer, Halloween, Christmas and academic half terms.

For example, the Easter campaign saw the first 'Giant golden egg hunt' which involved seeking out the location of the 20ft giant Easter egg placed on a famous landmark. A competition was launched offering prizes for correct entries.

During the busy summer months, visitors were entertained at the foot of the attraction with acrobatic performers to create a buzz among the crowds. The Halloween half-term holiday saw the introduction of the Creepy Cruise along the Thames, taking in the spooky sites of London with audio commentary and green-lit decks.

Meanwhile, adding to the Halloween experience at the London Eye, a Dracula on stilts, mummy entertainers and story-telling witches entertained children. Kids were encouraged to dress in scary costumes to take their Halloween flights and were offered 'trick or treat' goody bags, as well as a chance to enter a competition in the Ghastly Guide to London booklet.

The British Airways London Eye website continues to drive customer sales and traffic and has become the first port of call for information, facts and figures. Through the 'Kids on the Eye' section, children can recreate the London attraction, take a virtual interactive cruise along the Thames and submit pictures and stories about their experiences.

In the past year, the London Eye was awarded 'The World's Leading Attraction' at the 11th Annual World Travel Awards and 'Best Attraction for Group Visits – short visits' at the Group's Travel Awards.

What does the brand promise you?

The British Airways London Eye has four key brand values: to be inspiring, visionary, sophisticated and unique.

How was the brand developed?

The creators of the British Airways London Eye are husband and wife architects David Marks and Julia Barfield. The first drawings of the London Eye were made on their kitchen table in South London in 1993, when the couple had entered a competition to design a millennium landmark.

The competition was scrapped, but Marks and Barfield were convinced that their dream should be pursued. They began to piece the project together, soon attracting the attention of the London press. This led British Airways to become a partner.

Soon, everyone realised the sheer scale of what they were attempting. It would be the largest observation wheel ever built and the only cantilevered structure of its kind in the world. It would also be the largest structure ever hoisted into a vertical position in one operation.

Over 1,700 people in five countries would be involved in building it. The population of

an entire alpine village would test the embarkation procedures. Glass for the capsules would have to be double-curved and laminated.

Transportation of the components would take on a scale reminiscent of the building of the pyramids: delivery would have to be timed to co-ordinate with tides in the River Thames, so that large parts could be safely negotiated under London's bridges. Clearance under Southwark Bridge would be as little as 40cm.

One of the world's tallest floating cranes would be needed to lift the massive quarter sections of the rim onto eight temporary platforms floating on the river. Each of the 32 passenger capsules would have to be designed to be within the maximum width allowed on the French roads, over which they would make their way to the English Channel and up the Thames. And it would all happen in just 16 months....

Did you know?

Towering at 135 metres high, visitors can view up to 40km in each direction over some of the world's most famous sights including St Paul's Cathedral, the Palace of Westminster and Windsor Castle.

The British Airways London Eye is the world's tallest observation wheel.

On average the London Eye makes 8,000 rotations in one calendar year at a speed of 0.26 metres per second.

The 32 high-tech passenger capsules can carry over 20,000 visitors a day.

The 80 'spokes' of the London Eye use a total of 6km of cable – enough to run from Trafalgar Square to Canary Wharf in London.

Caboodle·bags

When mums go out and about with a baby, they have to carry a huge amount of equipment around with them, from nappies and food, to clean clothes and wipes – the 'whole caboodle'. Hence the existence of Caboodle Bags, which are designed to combine practical features, like useful pockets, with fashion and style for parents.

What is Caboodle Bags?

The Caboodle collection offers young families a range of different bags to help carry the different equipment that young babies need. The Original Caboodle Bag was designed in 1986 featuring a separate baby changing mat, which is made of washable towelling, and a range of organiser pockets. It has changed and improved since its launch and has remained a bestseller.

The Active Bag, which is particularly popular with dads, has added features such as an insulated bottle pocket and parent's organiser pocket. This was instantly popular when it was first launched in 2001 and remains so today. The wipe-clean bag has a unisex, cross-body strap, with a pocket for a mobile phone as well as a front pocket with purse, key clip and penholders for parents. There is also a separate section at the bottom for dirty nappies.

The insulated bottle pocket, organiser section and mobile phone pocket are also included in the Caboodle Charcoal bag

which is designed as a modern messenger-style bag.

Latest additions to the brand's portfolio include a new limited edition range which is a collection of five stylish and contemporary changing bags. They are practical but will also keep mum and baby looking fashionable when they're out and about.

The trendy designs include a matching changing mat, a 'grubby stuff' bag and lots of useful pockets, which are see-through to help busy parents find what they're looking for quickly. There are also leather-look loops to attach the bag to a pram. The new range comes in five different designs: Stripes and lines, Red heart, Jade buttons, Hessian and Black spot.

How was the brand developed?

Caboodle Bags founder Ruth Kirby-Smith, turned a simple idea into a successful business. She was a busy academic when she had her daughter, supervising students and running a large research contract.

One of the most important pieces of baby equipment was a bag for all of her daughter's equipment. She discovered there wasn't a good baby bag on the market, so was forced to buy a large shopping bag which had plenty of pockets.

When her son was born, Ruth took time out to spend with her babies and designed the baby bag which she would have liked to have. She noticed that there was a huge gap in the market for baby bags designed by women for women, as many of the existing bags had been designed by men.

So, Ruth designed the first Caboodle bag, a practical baby changing bag with separate changing mat, lots of pockets and sealable compartments. It was an immediate success. As young families' lives become more mobile, Caboodle Bags aims to help women organise their lives with a baby in an easy, practical way.

Ruth founded Caboodle Bags in 1986 and 20 years on the business has grown to become a well-established British brand. The company employs women, all who are able to fit their work around family needs. This ties into the company philosophy, which is all about putting family life first.

The full Caboodle range now includes the Limited Edition Range, Original Caboodle Bag, Caboodle Active, (which is targeted towards dads) and the Caboodle Bag. All are available in a number of designs and colours including navy, charcoal, black polyester, wipe clean and varying sizes. They all have multiple pockets, a grubby stuff section, and changing mat.

Did you know?

The Caboodle Bags brand name came out of the blue. Ruth was following a car on the motorway loaded up with mum, dad, kids and luggage. "Gosh, they are taking the whole caboodle", she thought, coining the name for the company and the product.

The Caboodle Welly Bag was designed by Peter Kirby-Smith in 1988 as the perfect storage answer for muddy welly boots. It was a runaway success and members of the aristocracy and a number of royal families see the Caboodle Welly bag as an essential accessory.

What does the brand promise you?

Caboodle Bags combines practical features with style. The range offers a wide variety of baby changing bags that are suitable for parents with busy lifestyles. The brand has built up a reputation among mothers and within the nursery industry for quality, service and reliability, all provided at a fair price.

Caboodle Bags is a brand that listens to what parents have to say and this is reflected in the products. Ruth Kirby-Smith, is still designing and selling Caboodle Bags 20 years after its launch. She has purposefully developed a company ethos flexible enough to allow employees to work for Caboodle while simultaneously bringing up their family.

CASIO.

Small is the new black. And while many consumer electronic companies have been recently leaping onto the bandwagon to shrink their products; CASIO has been focused on miniaturisation for decades.

This is one reason why CASIO products are such a hit with kids, they're often kid-sized, but most importantly they're simple to use too. In the UK, one in three calculators and one in three electronic keyboards sold every year is a CASIO.

What is CASIO?

CASIO is a Japanese electronics company, which manufactures calculators, electronic keyboards, watches and cameras. Its products appeal to kids, because they're simple to operate and easy to use.

CASIO calculators have always played a central role for kids at school, with two thirds of secondary school children using them for their studies. They are the only calculators on the market with a natural textbook display. They include everything else required by the current school curriculum and are recommended for use in all school examinations.

CASIO's digital cameras have a 'BESTSHOT' mode to help budding photographers improve their photos. Similarly, CASIO's key lighting keyboards enable fledgling pianists to learn and play a tune effortlessly. Meanwhile, its famously indestructible G-Shock and Baby-G watches are built to withstand all bumps and knocks in the playground.

Where would you have seen the brand?

In 2005, CASIO launched a new approach to forge closer, emotional bonds with its consumers and place emphasis on the CASIO brand above and beyond its products. The 'Casiology' approach has rolled out an integrated consumer campaign across advertising, brochures and point of sale material.

The mainstream advertising campaign was showcased in the national press, key lifestyle magazines, influential websites as well as a number of major city outdoor poster sites, and London Underground stations. The campaign was supported with further promotions in nightclubs, shopping centres and exhibition centres. The Casiology campaign was a huge success for the brand, boosting awareness by 8%, increasing appeal by 22% and consumer's propensity to purchase by 20%.

CASIO's crucial role in kids' education is reinforced by several corporate social responsibility initiatives. The brand is involved in training maths teachers to use digital technology in class, as a way of improving performance. It also conducted research in 2004, which showed that children want to learn more about maths and science, a project that received nationwide press coverage.

CASIO's products are distributed far and wide across every high street and shopping centre. Its range of watches, calculators, cameras and keyboards can be bought in major retailers, department stores and specialist stationery, jewellery, music and photographic shops.

How was the brand developed?

Nearly 50 years ago, Tadao Kashio, CASIO's Japanese founder saw an electronic motorised calculator the size of a desk at a trade fair. It was operated by gears and was extremely noisy and cumbersome. Kashio was convinced he could do better and started to develop his own calculating machine. In 1954, he created an electric calculator that weighed 30kg and was the size of a backpack.

Kashio grew up in a farming family in Nagoku City in Japan and loved creating things. Initially he founded a business to make aeroplane parts, but that was before he started creating calculators. His three brothers then joined his company to help create a better version of the CASIO calculator.

Although the Model 124-A calculator was eventually a major hit in Japan and overseas, it wasn't all plain sailing. On one occasion the brothers were due to unveil their new device to a prospective buyer but it wouldn't fit on the plane to make the journey to his offices. The brothers dismantled the machine but when they

What does the brand promise you?

A relentless quest for innovation has always been at the heart of the CASIO brand, led by its mantra which is, 'if it's not totally original, it's not CASIO'. CASIO is determined to remain one of the few brands that stimulates its consumers by constantly discovering newer and better ways of doing things.

CASIO is a brand that is guided by the Kashio brothers' philosophy of 'creativity and contribution'. This philosophy translates into three core brand values. First, trust – CASIO's products are high quality, good value and very rarely malfunction. Second, innovation – through both technology and function. Third, accessibility – CASIO's products are always easy-to-use, which is why they're popular with kids.

It will be CASIO's 50th anniversary in 2007 and over the last half century, it has created possibilities for its consumers. This is a brand whose expertise in personal technology aims to revolutionise its customers' personal and professional lives – just as Tadao Kashio dreamed of.

reassembled it at the end of the journey, it wouldn't work anymore.

Soon, rival manufacturers began to create their own calculators, which were smaller and easier to use than CASIO's model. In 1972, CASIO responded to its competition with the first electronic calculator.

The Japanese electronics company soon realised that its future lay not just with business, but with the man on the street too. It expanded its market by targeting affluent consumers who could afford to pay £80 for a product. In 1972, the CASIO mini was an immediate success and from then on CASIO focused on miniaturisation.

It wasn't long before CASIO was innovating beyond calculators. In 1975, it launched a digital watch called the Casiotron, which has since become a desirable collectors' item. Five years later, in January 1980, the company's first electronic musical instrument the Casiotone 201 was launched.

CASIO then applied its world-leading technology to developing pocket TVs and word processors for the Japanese market. More recently, CASIO has launched the world's first mass-market digital camera and the Cassiopeia, a hand-held PC.

Did you know?

In the last 10 years CASIO has sold more than two million G-Shock and Baby-G watches in the UK alone.

Two thirds of secondary school children use CASIO calculators for their studies.

In the UK, one in three calculators and one in three electronic keyboards sold every year is a CASIO.

CASIO is the official licensed Timepiece of the 2006 FIFA World Cup in Germany.

CASIO's Wave Ceptor watches check themselves for accuracy.

early learning centre

Early Learning Centre is a specialist toy shop for children aged 0-6 years, dedicated to helping children develop and learn through play. Its toys are designed to stimulate children's development in many ways – to help children explore the boundaries of their imaginations and creativity, to make learning fun and help children be all they can be.

The brand works closely with child development experts, from child psychologists and nursery school teachers to mums and children themselves, to design and create their products.

What is Early Learning Centre?

The heart of the Early Learning Centre brand is the products it sells and in reflection of the power and distinctiveness of the brand, 80% of sales are for its own branded products.

The product range is not only segmented by age group, but also by development area. The range breaks down into nine segments.

Firstly, Baby and Toddler consists of first toys to awaken the senses and encourage early exploration. Sport and Activity toys help children get active, strengthen muscles and help develop co-ordination. Learning is Fun – toys that encourage letter and number recognition and help prepare for school. Musical toys to help children express themselves and develop self-confidence fall into the Making Music category. Bookworm Corner which offers children an introduction into the world of reading, stories, knowledge and understanding. Puzzle it Out – fun puzzles and games to help children develop reasoning skills. Let's Pretend – imaginative toys that help children explore their identity and develop self-confidence. Action and Adventure – adventure toys that stretch the imagination and encourage group play and social skills. The final segment, Art and Creativity, includes drawing and painting materials as well as making toys that develop creativity and self-expression.

Early Learning Centre spends over £1 million a year on new product development and launches over 750 new toys every year.

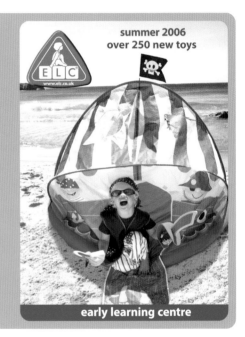
summer 2006
over 250 new toys

early learning centre

Where would you have seen the brand?

Early Learning Centre is one of the most familiar and respected brands on UK high streets, with 214 dedicated stores. It also supplies toys to be sold through leading stores such as Debenhams department stores, Sainsbury's and Boots the Chemist.

Early Learning Centre started life as a mail order business, and direct sales through the internet and catalogues have been strong in recent years. The website, www.elc.co.uk, was first launched in 1999 and proved such a success that it achieved full profitability in its first year and won New Media Age Best Retail Website in 2003. It was re-launched in

October 2005 with easier navigation, more in-depth information and a new fresh engaging look. Early Learning Centre also prints and distributes over four million catalogues in the UK each year.

Over the years Early Learning Centre has received countless awards for its innovative products. Recent awards include the Right Start Magazine 2005 gold award for Music which recognised Early Learning Centre's Keyboard & Stool. Its Cash Register won a platinum award from the Baby & Toddler Gear Guide 2005, and the Sizzlin' Kitchen won best value toy from the Prima Baby Reader Awards 2005. Early Learning Centre also won the Tommy's Parent Friendly Award 2005 for Best Toy Brand.

How was the brand developed?

Early Learning Centre was established in 1974 by John Beale. Like many great entrepreneurs, his idea was born out of a personal frustration – he simply couldn't find sufficiently inspiring toys for his own children. This was his inspiration to create a toy business that would inspire and stimulate children to develop as they played.

Initially the business was based on a book club model, whereby customers were sent a monthly selection of toys to try out with their children and then choose what to keep or return. This principle of enabling customers to try products with their children before purchase is still important to Early Learning Centre today.

What does the brand promise you?

The Early Learning Centre brand is about child development and fun. It believes that when children are playing with the right kind of toys, play can be enormously beneficial and help every child to explore their own potential in their own way. Indeed, this insight provides the binding glue for consumers who find Early Learning Centre the best choice of toys for their children.

Indeed, stores are unique in encouraging customers to take products out of boxes so that their children can experience playing with them before a decision is made to purchase. Early Learning Centre stores still devote every Tuesday morning to 'Playtime' when customers are invited to play with lots of new toys and join in organised activities and competitions.

By 1980 the business had 10 stores across the country, growing to 90 stores four years later. There are now 214 stores with a programme of store refurbishments currently underway, aimed at creating an inviting, inspiring and interactive retail environment for children and parents to enjoy spending time in.

The packaging is also undergoing change and includes developmental icons to help parents understand the key skill that each toy provides to help their child develop. There are also 'Play-tips' on each pack that give parents some helpful ideas on how to get the most out of playing with their children.

Early Learning Centre is stepping up its commitment to developing cutting edge unique products that are designed around the development needs of children. Every month, an innovation team, that includes designers and leading experts in child development, creates new product ideas.

Did you know?

The Chairman, Tim Waterstone, should certainly know his product – he has eight children. The youngest is 11, the eldest 42.

Early Learning Centre's best-selling item for Christmas 2005 was its keyboard & stool – over 75,000 were sold.

Early Learning Centre has sold 5.5 million playballs – that's enough to fill 10 Olympic Sized swimming pools.

There's nothing like a camping holiday to provide fun for the whole family. But, imagine the pleasure of going camping without having to wrestle with a tent or tow a caravan across the continent. And that's what Eurocamp is about: living in the great outdoors without the hassle. This is a holiday company that has put the luxury back into outdoor living. But more importantly over 30 years experience in camping has taught Eurocamp that entertaining the kids is the best way to ensure a relaxing, enjoyable holiday for the whole family.

What is Eurocamp?

Eurocamp is the leading tour operator for European camping holidays. Every year, more than 130,000 people choose a Eurocamp holiday, staying in mobile homes, tents and chalets across Europe. From France and Croatia to Switzerland and Sardinia, Eurocamp offers accommodation in over 150 holiday parcs across 12 European countries and islands. Eurocamp offers a range of accommodation in three bedroom tents, spacious mobile homes or European-style chalets. It's not camping as you know it, because it's complete with comforts ranging from air-conditioning to coffee makers and double beds to decking.

Where would you have seen Eurocamp?

Eurocamp's brand has always interacted directly with consumers and its holidays are not available via travel agents. Its brochure and website are the most important communication channels with prospective holiday makers. It sends out over 200,000 brochures every year leading consumers to book their holidays through the dedicated call centre or online at www.eurocamp.co.uk.

Eurocamp is the only brand in the camping sector that uses TV as a regular advertising channel. TV adverts normally appear on Christmas Eve on ITV, five and key satellite channels and run for two months to cover the most important booking period.

Eurocamp's 2006 TV campaign features an animated family developed by the Parisian team behind Hollywood blockbusters The Matrix and Harry Potter. Through animation the advert brings to life a young girl's memory of a Eurocamp holiday, from swimming to playing outdoors, all projected onto a real-life background.

TV advertising is supported by an online marketing and affinity programme, including a new selection of video footage from its parcs plus a mini-movie. Over 30,000

people viewed these in the first two weeks of January. Post holiday questionnaires and regular customer focus groups ensure Eurocamp keeps up to date with its customers. The family holiday group consistently achieves high scores in customer satisfaction surveys with overall satisfaction at 87% and intention to recommend rates now at 81%.

Eurocamp has twice won the prestigious Tommy's award, for best overseas tour operator in 2000 and the best parent-friendly holiday operator award in 1997. It has also won awards for its brochure and website in the 1998 and 2000 Guardian Travel Awards.

How was the brand developed?

Eurocamp was launched in 1973 when Alan Goulding began offering camping holidays to Brittany. Uniquely, it allowed holidaymakers to enjoy a camping holiday without the hassle of having to transport all the necessary camping equipment with them. Instead, everything was provided by Eurocamp, set up and ready for campers to use upon arrival.

From modest beginnings, the company grew strongly in the 1970s – fuelled in part by the growing British interest in all things French. The 1980s saw the Eurocamp brand mature. It was sold by its founder and mobile homes and parcs outside France were added to its portfolio.

Following a flotation on the London Stock Exchange in 1991, Eurocamp plc has grown to become the core brand of the renamed holding company, Holidaybreak plc, one of Europe's leading specialist holiday companies.

Its brand now offers chalets as well as mobile homes and tents to holidaymakers. It has also expanded to provide holidays across Europe in 12 countries and islands including France, Switzerland, Croatia, Germany, Austria, Spain and Italy. In 2002, Eurocamp grew further when it acquired rival camping company Eurosites.

What does the brand promise you?

The Eurocamp experience places kids at the centre of everything. It runs more than 750 hours of free childrens' clubs during the summer and offers other child-friendly services such as play tents, toddler-friendly parcs and a baby sitting service. Other facilities on the parcs include swimming pools, waterslides and mini golf and loads of open space. Eurocamp offers wide ranging entertainment for its junior holidaymakers with Fun Station providing a good opportunity for kids to make friends and give their parents a well-deserved break.

There are seven different kids' clubs from the Mini Fun Station for toddlers to Base for teenagers. For kids in-between, there's Leo's Fun Station for kids from four to six years; Fun Station 7+ which offers talent shows and poster designing, while Fun Station 10+ entertains older kids with team games and scavenger hunts.

Eurocamp has also named 57 of its parcs as toddler friendly. This means that they're a generally quieter and safer environment for toddlers, away from hazards like main roads, railways, steep ditches and water.

To help families holiday in style, Eurocamp provides highchairs, cot/play pens, and all-terrain buggies and rumble trucks to get around. Eurocamp's super junior tents can also be pitched next to tents or mobile homes for kids to have their own space to play in.

In a first for the camping industry, Eurocamp has also launched a special arrival survival service for its lone parent family customers. This alleviates the stress of the start of the holiday by helping them unpack and settle into their accommodation. The brand also offers all lone parent families a discount on its holidays.

Eurocamp has grown into a multi-million pound holiday brand that offers families a camping holiday, without the hassle. It's a brand that understands that life is for living.

Did you know?

Eurocamp buys over 27,000 teaspoons every year, so that holidaymakers can have a cup of tea, without having to worry about packing a teaspoon.

It gets through 294,000 tent pegs a year, so 'Eurocampers' don't have to worry about putting up and packing away their tent.

Eurocamp also buys 86,000 pillows plus blankets for its mobile homes and tents so there's no need to take a sleeping bag.

Eurocamp runs more than 750 hours of free childrens' clubs during the summer months.

Almost 12,500 people apply each year to be one of the 1,500 Eurocamp on parc representatives.

731 years is the combined service length of Eurocamp's experienced call centre staff.

GEOMAG is a magnetic construction toy. The brand is founded on the principles of the planet's two magnetic poles, which inspires its brand name. GEO stands for the planet earth, whereas MAG refers to magnetism.

The brand plays a number of different roles. It's an interesting play object but it's also a useful teaching aid for children learning about geometry, magnetism, mathematics or chemistry. GEOMAG can also help kids understand mechanical or atomic molecular structures.

What is GEOMAG?

GEOMAG is an intuitive, creative construction toy based around the principles of magnetism. It consists of a series of plastic-coated bars each with a north and south magnetic pole. The rods can be simply connected together using nickel-plated steel spheres.

GEOMAG is a toy for both boys and girls and has a broad appeal from six year-olds all the way up to adults. GEOMAG created a new category in the market with the launch of its magnetic construction toys. The brand has since grown and remains the market leader in this field.

The GEOMAG rods come in a number of different colours and finishes from metallic, to rods that glow in the dark. The toy also provides plastic panel accessories to help children build a vast range of structures. GEOMAG Panels are transparent geometrical shapes available in blue, green, red and yellow. They can be inserted into the GEOMAG structure of rods and spheres to build more

Astonishing New Products
Innovation & Best Quality

GEOMAG

Booth#2827 - Level 3 - Javis Center NY - Feb 20-23, 2005

www.geomagsa.com

complex structures such as castles, towers, bridges and other fantasy structures.

The panels enable children to use a smaller number of rods and spheres while building their GEOMAG structures. For example, it's possible to build a sphere with only rods by using 120 pieces, whereas the introduction of panels means only 60 pieces are needed. The shape of the panels mean children can build dynamic

structures, as every panel has a hole in the middle, through which it's possible to insert a rod and attach other panels to create moving pieces.

New products include GEOMAG DekoPanels, which enables children to personalise their constructions by inserting their own pictures or photos into the structure to make a 3D montage. Each DekoPanels box comes with stencils to shape and prepare the image and special software which can rotate, resize and copy images so they fit the panels, and then all they need to do is print and cut them out.

Other extensions to the range include the GEOMAG Dynamic Line to help children build 10 different rotating or moving models. GEOMAG Pastelles Panels is a fusion of fashionable, pastel-coloured rods and panels for more creative constructions. The new products come in packages of 46 or 84 piece sets and were inspired by the success of GEOMAG Panels, which was awarded the 2004/05 Toy of the Year by many organisations including Toty 2005 and Hamley's Best Toy Award – category Gold Award Winner.

Where would you have seen the brand?

GEOMAG sells its products in over 23 countries through leading distributors and affiliate companies. Its products can also be bought through the internet via various online retailers. Since GEOMAG's launch, several other companies have entered the magnetic toy market attempting to copy its system; however the brand is patented and legally protected.

GEOMAG has won numerous awards for its toys. In 2004/5, in the construction category, it won both The Good Toy Guide Silver Award and Right Start Best Toy Gold Award. In the same year, it won the Hamley's Best Toy in the category of Wonderland Toys.

GEOMAG Panels has also won a number of awards. It became the Toy of the Year in the US in 2005 and in the same year was awarded by the Duracell European Toy Survey, the Good Toy Guide, the Parent's Choice Foundation and the National Parenting Publications Award.

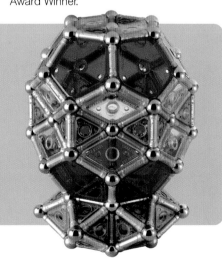

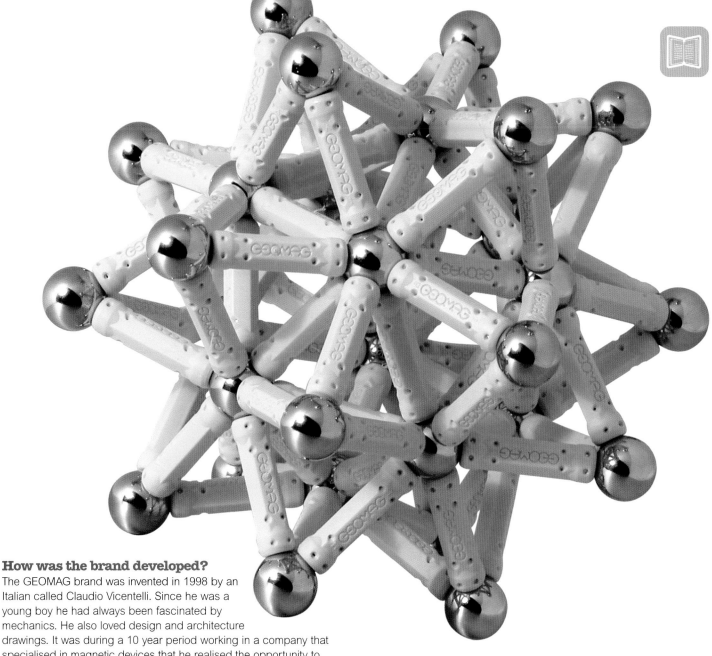

How was the brand developed?

The GEOMAG brand was invented in 1998 by an Italian called Claudio Vicentelli. Since he was a young boy he had always been fascinated by mechanics. He also loved design and architecture drawings. It was during a 10 year period working in a company that specialised in magnetic devices that he realised the opportunity to invent a magnetic toy for children.

He initially considered magnetically-linked bricks, but then he realised that the combination of magnetic bars and steel spheres would give children greater creative freedom. The products were then licensed and distributed by an Italian company. When its license expired in 2003, a new Swiss company called GEOMAG was launched to distribute its products.

What does the brand promise you?

GEOMAG aims to grow awareness and understanding of magnetism through entertaining tools based on fun, developing creativity and stimulating learning for all ages, using materials and production of the highest Swiss quality. GEOMAG hopes to help children answer the questions surrounding the phenomena of everyday life. It can help to inform children who want to learn more about magnetic attraction, the description of the earth as a giant magnet and the mysteries governing magnetic fields.

Did you know?

Between 2003 and 2005, the rods sold by GEOMAG could cover the distance from Dublin to New York.

Between 2004 and 2005, the panels sold by GEOMAG could cover 22 football fields.

In 2004/5, 46 million rods were sold in over 25 different countries.

Graco is one of the world's leading nursery goods brands. It is best known for its pushchairs and travel systems for babies, which include products such as Mosaic and Mirage and the best-selling Quattro Tour Deluxe. Graco prides itself on being responsible for a number of innovations for young families such as the travel cot.

What is Graco?

Graco is renowned for making easy to use, innovative products that are excellent value for money. Graco invented the 'travel system', the travel cot and the electronic swing. Graco's range also includes pushchairs, car seats, high chairs, swings, baby carriers, accessories and playpens, as well as bouncers, walkers and entertainers. Today Graco has grown to become the leading supplier of travel systems, travel cots and swings in the UK.

One of the brand's flagship products is the Mosaic travel system. This is a light pushchair plus AutoBaby car seat that locks onto the pushchair with one click and enables sleeping babies to be transported easily without disturbing them. It folds up compactly with an umbrella style fold and has brakes that push on/off – a great favourite with new mums.

Another popular, long-running product in the Graco range is the Mirage pushchair, suitable for young babies up to three years-old. It is compatible with the AutoBaby car seat and includes three recline positions, a play tray, a protective padded canopy with window and front suspension. The Mirage has been winning awards since its launch in 1997.

Where would you have seen the brand?

Graco is widely available from retailers on the high street such as Mothercare, Toys R Us, Halfords, John Lewis, ASDA and Argos as well as leading independent retailers. Its promotional strategy includes consumer PR and advertising in key parenting titles, a presence in retail catalogues as well as in-store promotion and an in-store training academy.

In the UK, the brand's marketing is focused around the consumer parenting press. Graco has been advertising in these magazines since its UK launch. It also runs regular competitions in these magazines.

This year, Graco launched a new marketing campaign called 'Mums Who Know Go Graco', which focuses on real mums talking about the brand. This theme will run across all advertising and promotional campaigns throughout 2006, as well as packaging and POS. Mums Who Know is more than an ad campaign, Graco is also feeding the mums' information back into its research and development team.

PR has also played an essential role in building the brand's awareness and reputation. For the last five years Graco has been central in organising The Travel Safe campaign alongside Mother & Baby magazine and retailer Halfords. The PR campaign aims to raise awareness about the importance of correctly-fitted car seats for children, as research has shown that over 80% of car seats are fitted incorrectly.

Every summer, Graco Training Academy expert John Thompson takes the Travel Safe Road Show to selected Halfords stores across the UK. Parents bring along their car seats so that Graco's experts can check the fit. Thanks in part to this campaign, the Government is proposing new legislation for children's car seats that will come into force by September 2006.

Graco is also a regular winner of product testing awards run by the consumer press including Best Buy and Best Value awards from Mother & Baby, Pregnancy & birth, Prima Baby, Practical Parenting and Baby & Toddler Gear culminating in a Gold award in 2004 and Silver award in 2005 at the Mother & Baby Awards.

How was the brand developed?

Graco is a global brand that has been in existence for nearly 60 years. However, in 1942, when Graco Metal Products was launched in Philadelphia, US it did not make products for babies. In the first 11 years of its life, Graco made machine and car parts for local manufacturers. When one of the founders left, the remaining partner decided to make his own line of products.

At that time, David Saint worked as an engineer and stained glass artisan for the brand. He was a father of nine children and had often watched his wife soothe a tired baby with a swing in their backyard. Inspired by what he saw, he went to the drawing board and 18 months later the world's first wind-up infant swing, the Graco Swyngomatic®, was born.

From then on, Graco was a brand in the baby products business. And after selling millions of Swyngomatics, Graco launched further innovations. In 1987, the brand's Pack N' Play®, a portable playpen and travel cot in one, was designed by Nate Saint, the son of the Swyngomatic's inventor, with great success. The following decade saw Graco introduce the Travel System, the first product to allow parents to move their sleeping babies from home to car to pushchair in one click.

Graco Europe was launched in September 1997 and has grown to become the number one wheeled goods manufacturer and number two car seat manufacturer in the UK (Source: FSA). In 1998, Graco acquired Century Car Seats combining the two brands under the Graco flag and has since produced award-winning concepts like the AutoBaby 0+ car seat, the first one-click in-car SafetyBase and the RallySport high-backed booster seat. The innovation continues in 2006, with the launch of the TriLogic range of car seats under the strap line 'The Science of Safety'.

Did you know?

The Graco Swyngomatic, the world's first wind-up infant swing, went on sale in 1943.

What does the brand promise you?

Graco is a trustworthy and reliable brand that places its consumers at the heart of its business. It is a progressive and dynamic company that aims to make life easier for new parents by offering a product range that's easy to use, innovative, safe and excellent value for money.

Great Little Trading Co. is a specialty catalogue and online retailer for families with children from 0-12. The company's aim is simple: to make a parent's life easier by providing a wide range of practical and hard-to-find products, with the convenience of round-the-clock ordering and home or office delivery.

What is Great Little Trading Co.?

Great Little Trading Co.'s customers are busy, because that's what happens when you're raising a young family, so the brand places emphasis on convenience. It simplifies the shopping experience by providing high quality, good value products delivered direct to the home. Great Little Trading Co. does not operate on the high street because it believes its parents favour convenient home shopping, and because its range is too big to be easily presented in a high street format.

Great Little Trading Co. offers an extensive range of products for the whole family, from safety products to skiwear, toy storage and personalised Christmas gifts. The brand works hard to find good quality products from all over the world, things that can be difficult to find elsewhere.

All products are tested by family and friends to ensure they meet the needs of parents and kids. This helps customers trust the products that they select.

In an increasingly competitive environment it is very important to develop and source innovative, parent-friendly products. Great Little Trading Co. appreciates how much parents care about what they buy for their children – they want the best for their children, and want to spend their money wisely. Over the last 10 years, the brand has established its position as a trusted guide.

Where would you have seen the brand?

Great Little Trading Co. mails over three million catalogues a year throughout the UK. Its website runs in parallel, taking 60% of all orders.

Increasingly the web is becoming an important customer recruitment channel and Great Little Trading Co. works closely with many parenting websites. Email shots,

including email reminders for children's birthdays, form a key part of the overall marketing mix. The brand also works with parenting magazines to drive awareness.

In 2001, Great Little Trading Co. won Best All Round Catalogue Business in its turnover bracket at the mail order industry awards (ECMOD). The exceptional growth of the business led to Great Little Trading Co. being listed in the top 100 fastest growing companies in the UK (Deloitte & Touché Indy 100).

How was the brand developed?

The company was founded in September 1995 by Alyssa Lovegrove and Caroline Clark, both professional working women with young families of their own. At the time, the Great Little Trading Co. catalogue was groundbreaking in the UK because it defined a new concept: practical household products specifically for families with young children. Initially they offered customers 150 products; it now has over 1,500.

Since its launch, the company has grown at an average annual rate of 50% with a current turnover of just over £11 million. This success is attributed to the brand's

What does the brand promise you?

Great Little Trading Co. promises its consumers a 'Great Little Difference...' to other shopping experiences. It is aware that its customers want the very best for their children, which is what it strives to deliver. It endeavours to source products from all over the world that can't be found anywhere else.

The brand also places emphasis on advice and service. For example, the catalogue and website use unique symbols to give clear guidance on product characteristics such as age compatibility. Service commitment is typified by the company's platinum delivery service where large furniture items are delivered by a two-man service at a convenient time, to the room of the customer's choice.

Great Little Trading Co. always makes an effort to listen to its customers' feedback and suggestions. Every year a series of 'Mums' Forums' are held with customers to seek suggestions about how to develop the service and range. The company works hard to implement customer ideas: for example, the hardwearing, cotton kids' pyjamas returned to the range after customer feedback revealed how much they were missed.

values and its appealing product range – much of which is exclusive.

In its product selection, Great Little Trading Co. is seeking to extend, rather than compete with, the range offered by large high street retailers. From the start, the brand has consistently sought out products which more traditional retailers are unwilling to develop or stock.

The emphasis is on innovative, practical and convenience-driven products, many of which come from abroad. This focus on design and innovation is what distinguishes Great Little Trading Co. from its competitors, and what has generated a loyal customer following.

It currently offers a selection of practical products for young families, under the

heading of 'clever ideas' such as a seat-belt cushion for sleepy children on car journeys and a duvet clip to keep kids' bedding in place at night. Other parts of the range include educational toys to stimulate their children's development; health and safety aids and parenting books to help parents create a safe and nurturing environment; and travel accessories and recreational equipment for use on the go.

The range also extends to bedroom furnishings, kitchen equipment and other convenient household items. Storage specifically for kids' toys and accessories is an area where Great Little Trading Co. leads the market. It also offers different gifts that can be personalised with a child's name, photograph or artwork.

Did you know?

Great Little Trading Co. has helped 40,000 parents get a good night's sleep with its bunny alarm clock, for children who can't yet tell the time. Children know it's not time to get up until the sleeping bunny wakes.

During autumn and winter, it sells over 50 different products which can be personalised with a child's name.

Great Little Trading Co.'s buying team travels the equivalent of six times around the world every year, to source the most innovative products for its catalogue.

grobag® is the specialist baby sleeping brand. All of its products are associated with baby sleep with a priority placed on baby safety. The brand is best known for the grobag baby sleeping bag, which is a 'wearable' blanket. This means that it can't be kicked off in the night or slip over a baby's head and cause overheating.

What is grobag?

grobag baby sleeping bags were developed to aid a safe and comfortable night's sleep for babies, and peace of mind for parents. The brand was designed with an emphasis on safety, following advice from the Foundation for the Study of Infant Deaths (FSID) and stringent testing criteria.

The company believes that grobag can make a difference to a good night's sleep for both babies and therefore their parents. The grobag baby sleeping bag range comes in a wide variety of designs with a choice of fabric, size and tog ratings, which helps parents determine the correct warmth.

The grobag products always include detailed information and advice on how to use the baby sleeping bag safely, with a set of easy-to-understand illustrations that demonstrate the brand's benefits. Each product also comes with a free nursery thermometer to help parents monitor the baby room's temperature.

Innovation plays a crucial role for grobag, and several new features have been added to the baby sleeping bags since its launch. These include the 'zip-click' which is designed to stop adventurous babies from opening the zips of their sleeping bags.

Similarly, a travel version of the grobag has been launched, which is suitable for use in a car seat or cot. Additionally, the brand has extended into other baby products that promote safe sleep. These include the grobag egg – a colour-changing digital thermometer – and the grobag socksuit, which is designed to overcome some of the problems of badly-fitting sleep suits.

The brand is now available to consumers through a mixture of different retail channels, such as independent nursery shops, major nursery retailers, mail order and through their own web company Bump to 3. Today, despite increased competition, independent market research has found that grobag remains the most popular baby sleeping bag in the UK.

Where would you have seen the brand?

The marketing of the grobag brand has played a crucial role in developing awareness of the concept of baby sleeping bags. The brand is supported by both consumer and trade advertising, primarily appearing in mainstream consumer parenting magazines. Additionally, twice a year the grobag safe sleep products are showcased to parents and nursery retailers at the Harrogate Nursery Fair and the Baby and Child Fair at the NEC.

The grobag brand has also won a number of awards which have helped to boost awareness of the brand. For example, in 2005 grobag collected a Mother & Baby magazine gold award for 'Best Nursery Item' for the second year running, FQ magazine 'Top Gear' gold award for the grobag egg and a Parent Friendly Award from the children's charity Tommy's.

How was the brand developed?

The idea of grobag baby sleeping bags was born from real-life experience. The founders of the brand, Rob and Ouvrielle Holmes discovered that their nine month old son, Sam, was constantly kicking off his covers, leading him to wake up through the night.

Exhausted from sleep deprivation, the couple's Austrian sister-in-law recommended a baby sleeping bag,

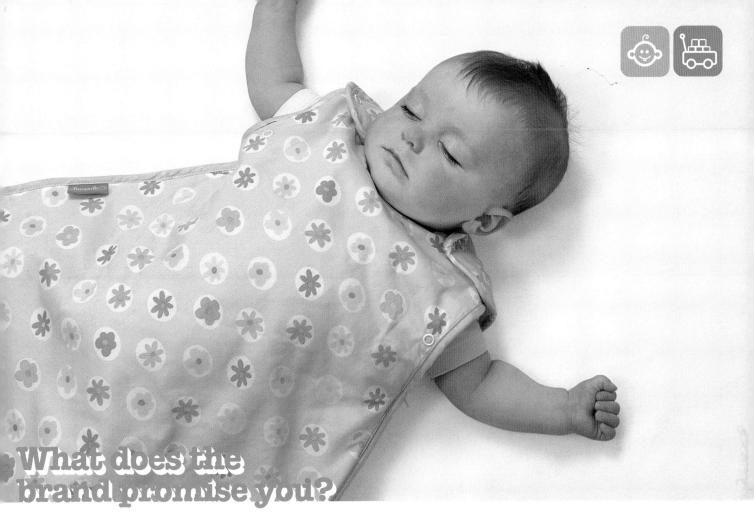

What does the brand promise you?

Put simply, the grobag brand promise a safe and sound night's sleep for babies and the peace of mind that brings for parents. grobag is regarded as a brand that has pioneered safe sleep. It is trusted by parents because of the priority it places on baby safety.

The grobag brand believes it understands the needs of parents and strives to make their lives easier. By helping to keep sleeping babies safe and secure, grobag aims to reassure parents. Safety, innovation and comfort are the three brand values at the heart of grobag.

which, as it turns out, was normal for babies in many parts of Europe. After the first night in his sleeping bag, Sam slept for 12 hours and his parents were hooked.

Realising the commercial possibilities of introducing baby sleeping bags to the UK, they began an intensive period of product research and created the grobag brand. To ensure grobag was as safe as possible, they worked with the Foundation for the Study of Infant Deaths (FSID), which helped them gain credibility and reassure new customers.

When the brand was launched in September 2000 at the Earl's Court Baby Show, the concept of baby sleeping bags was almost unknown in the UK. Grobag sold 1,000 sleeping bags in three hours and had sold out by lunchtime on the first day of the show. One of the retailers visiting the stand asked founder Rob Holmes how long grobag had been in business. He looked at his watch, and replied, "about four hours now!"

Since the brand's successful launch, the range has expanded into other baby sleep-related products and is now marketed and sold worldwide. In 2004, the company was re-branded and restructured to launch the international distribution company gro-group, which distributes other baby products as well as grobag – the main brand in the company's expanding portfolio.

Did you know?

The company estimates that it now sells one grobag baby sleeping bag every 60 seconds.

The inspiration for the original grobag logo was taken from the founder's second child Lucy, who used to wear her hair in a top knot hairstyle. Despite various tweaks of the logo over the years, the happy sleeping baby and top knot has remained.

In the early years, the company was run from small offices above a nightclub (another Holmes family business), where lack of sleep was par for the course. It was an ideal location for matchmaking couples who might eventually create potential future grobag customers.

Haliborange is a leading children's healthcare brand. It produces a range of health supplements, which are aimed specifically at children. Haliborange provides parents with an option to ensure their children obtain the recommended intake of nutrients, as part of a healthy diet.

What is Haliborange?

Children need to have a balance of vitamins, minerals and Omega-3 fatty acids to ensure maximum growth and development. Every parent wants the best for their child to give them the best head start in life.

Children's nutritional intake can be related to their mental performance and concentration. Children can be notoriously fussy eaters and as a result miss out on important nutrients. Fruit-flavoured health supplements, Haliborange's forte, are therefore often perceived to be the easiest, tastiest way of adding to the body's supplies of vitamins, minerals and Omega-3 nutrients effectively.

Haliborange produces a range of fruit flavoured health supplements, which combines Omega-3 fish oil and important vitamins. Research has shown that young brains require certain nutrients, including Omega-3, to develop to their maximum potential. Omega-3 is found naturally in fish oil, and is thought to help in physical as well as mental development and aid a child's concentration and therefore their ability to learn.

Where would you have seen the brand?

This vitamin and mineral brand has a rich heritage and many people remember Haliborange fondly from their childhood. To support its retail customers and inform and educate consumers, Haliborange invests heavily in product and brand promotion.

A £3 million campaign for the Haliborange Omega-3 for Kids product

using terrestrial and satellite TV was aired in 2005. The TV spots are backed by national press advertising and posters to increase visibility of the brand. The key message of the campaign is: 'Haliborange Omega-3 Smart Thinking for Children.' In addition these messages are reflected on in-store promotions.

The growth of Haliborange Omega-3 has also been driven by a public relations campaign where the products were tested in schools with great success. Haliborange also invests in training pharmacy staff in order to help educate and inform consumers of the Omega-3 for Kids' benefits.

How was the brand developed?

Haliborange dates back to the 1930s when it was marketed as the: 'Nicest way of taking Halibut Liver Oil.' At that time children were given fish oil supplements to provide vitamins A, C and D. Haliborange prided itself in the fresh juicy orange flavour and the fact the syrup had no fishy taste.

The introduction of fish oil supplements providing vitamins A, C and D under the Welfare Food Scheme in the early 1940s led to an almost complete abolition of

childhood rickets, which is a disease caused by a deficiency of vitamin D. In fact, fish oil liquid was distributed free to pregnant and nursing mothers and children up to five years old through the Ministry of Food's Welfare Food programme – a product endorsement that has never been surpassed in healthcare's history.

The Government still recommends that vitamins A, C and D supplements should be given to infants and young children up to five years and it provides vitamin drops to mothers free of charge.

In the 1950s, Haliborange produced the first compressed tablet containing these vitamins. This was one of the first flavoured chewable tablets that made it easier for children to take their daily vitamin pill.

Over the years Haliborange developed a range of fruit-flavoured, chewable vitamins. These expanded to include vitamin C tablets with calcium and iron, which are important minerals for growing teenagers, as well as multivitamin syrups suitable for children under three.

Since 2000, the supplement market for Omega-3 has had a meteoric rise following scientific evidence establishing the link between children's brain development and Omega-3 fish oil. It has led Haliborange to return to its roots and once again provide fish oil formulas for children through its Omega-3 Fish Oil for Kids range.

Haliborange has continued to extend its Omega-3 for Kids range following the success of the Haliborange Omega-3 for Kids Syrup and its Orange Chewy Fruit Bursts. Haliborange Omega-3 for Kids is the best selling Omega-3 supplement on the market (Source: IR December 2005).

Today, around 17 million people take supplements regularly in the UK. Haliborange is the fastest growing and the second largest brand behind Seven Seas in the vitamin and mineral supplement market.

What does the brand promise you?

Haliborange is a trusted, family-oriented brand with a long heritage of providing good health naturally. Haliborange is committed to developing and marketing evidence-based, innovative health products. Its range is clearly differentiated, providing innovative solutions for the family's health protection.

Did you know?

Haliborange was named after its ingredients. Its first product was made from halibut oil and orange juice.

Haliborange was also nicknamed the 'Sunshine Vitamin' because it contained vitamin D whose chief source is from sunlight on uncovered skin.

The fish oil used in Haliborange Omega-3 comes from cod and tuna. Both are in plentiful supply as they're specially selected from well-managed fishing grounds around the world.

Omega-3 fatty acids have been shown to help maintain a healthy heart, supple and flexible joints as well as more recently being heralded for their brain development benefits.

HARIBO®

HARIBO®'s iconic gum and jelly sweets have a unique taste and texture and are made in fun, colourful designs.

HARIBO is a bright, happy, fun and friendly brand, demonstrated by its famous slogan: 'Kids and grown-ups love it so, the happy world of HARIBO.' The brand is easily recognisable, thanks to its eye-catching logo and the iconic image of the Hariboy® that appeals to all age groups.

What is HARIBO?

HARIBO is the world's largest gums and jellies manufacturer and the market leader in the UK with over 25% market share (Source: IRI, October 1st 2005 – volume share). Its flagship sub-brand is Starmix®, a mix of fruit-flavour and sweet foam gums, which have grown over the last 10 years to a retail value of over £30 million. HARIBO's other top-selling sweets include Tangfastics® and Kiddies Super Mix®.

HARIBO's primary focus is gums and jellies but it also produces fruit chews, which includes the MAOAM® range of Mao Mix®, MAOAM Stripes and MAOAM Minis, as well as liquorice and marshmallows.

Its portfolio includes brands such as Strawbs, Goldbears®, Happy Cola®, Jelly Babies, Wine Gums, Jelly Beans, Horror Mix®, Fizzy Cola, Milky Mix, Chamallows® and Liquorice Twists, to name a few.

HARIBO's products come in various bag sizes, drums and can also be bought loose in bulk. On the high street, HARIBO sweets are sold in mini bags for kids to buy with their pocket money, adult sizes to share at work, or in party packs and gift boxes, to name just a few formats.

The latest addition to the HARIBO portfolio is Starlets®, a product which was launched in autumn 2005. The sweet has a crunchy sugar-coated exterior shell with a fruit gum centre and comes in seven different flavours.

Another successful 2005 launch is HARIBO Strawbs, which has grown from zero to over £1.8 million in retail value (Source: IRI, October 1st 2005 – value sales). It is a strawberry-shaped jelly sweet containing real fruit juice.

HARIBO is the most well-known brand within the total sugar confectionery

market. When prompted, 94% of children and adults had heard of HARIBO (Source: Resolution Research, January 2004).

Where would you have seen the brand?

HARIBO products can be found in a wide variety of retailers from large supermarkets to smaller shops like the local corner shop or convenience store and from garden and leisure centres to fashion stores.

The brand is supported with a marketing budget of over £5 million and is promoted through all communication channels including TV, online, PR, events, direct marketing, sponsorship and sampling.

HARIBO has been advertising on TV for over 11 years based on its core slogan: 'Kids and grown ups love it so, the happy world of HARIBO.' Although the latest TV ad supports the launch of the new Starlets product, HARIBO also runs umbrella TV campaigns to support its entire product portfolio.

Event marketing plays a strategic role in HARIBO's promotional strategy, by involving consumers directly with new experiences. The Kids Rule event is a once in a lifetime opportunity for a team of kids to run the HARIBO sweets factory. There is a national search to find 10 children to take over factory roles for a day, including the chance to be on the panel of sweet tasters. It is a multilayered campaign with national media involvement. Birthdays also offer an opportunity for HARIBO's event marketing. Children are offered the chance to win their birthday party courtesy of the brand.

The HARIBO website offers a range of interactive games for kids and grown-ups alike, including monthly competitions. Additionally, there are HARIBO Perimeter boards at three Premiership football grounds.

Sampling is an important channel for the brand to increase awareness. A HARIBO 4x4 Truck travels across the UK visiting different events, from retail outlets to concerts and universities, with samples for visitors giving them the opportunity to try the product.

The HARIBO Kids Club is a useful direct marketing tool to strengthen consumer loyalty. Currently, the club has over 9,000 members in the UK. Kids of all ages can join for a nominal annual fee, in return for regular mailings, presents and an opportunity to taste the latest HARIBO products first.

What does the brand promise you?

HARIBO's brand mission is 'to provide high quality treats for kids that taste so delicious, even grown-ups can't resist'.

How was the brand developed?

In 1920, a young German confectioner called Hans Riegel made sweets in his Bonn kitchen, which were then delivered to shops by his wife on an old bicycle. Today HARIBO is still family-run, but has grown from a German kitchen to 18 production sites worldwide and exports to over 105 countries.

HARIBO entered the UK market in 1972, when it acquired a majority stake in the English firm Dunhills (Pontefract), whose famous round liquorice Pontefract Cakes are still produced today. In 1994 HARIBO acquired the remaining shares in Dunhills.

While ensuring that the traditions of Dunhills were maintained, HARIBO introduced its own production and

packaging methods as well as new recipes which improved the product quality.

HARIBO focused its efforts on developing the appeal of gums and jellies among children, launching novelty gum and jelly shapes in drums to be sold as single pieces and introducing a range of HARIBO branded bag 'mixes' containing a selection of novelty shapes.

In 1995 HARIBO's first nationwide TV commercial dramatically increased awareness of the brand. HARIBOY, who had already featured on all HARIBO bags, suddenly became a celebrity by appearing in HARIBO's TV advertising campaigns and at a variety of children's events throughout the UK.

Did you know?

The brand name spells out the founder and his town: HAns RIegel, BOnn – HARIBO.

90 million HARIBO Heart Throbs are produced every month.

Standing side by side, the number of HARIBO Goldbears produced in a year would circle the earth 3.5 times.

Goldbears were the favourite sweet of Albert Einstein.

HARIBO fans include Prince William, Amanda Holden, Richard Bacon, Claire Sweeny, Sadie Frost and Kate Winslet.

Heinz Spaghetti is an iconic UK brand that has been loved by kids and their parents for over 75 years. The brand enables parents to encourage kids to eat wholesome food because, as well as being fun to eat, it contains no artificial colours, preservatives or flavours.

What is Heinz Spaghetti?

Heinz Spaghetti is a tinned food product made from durum wheat pasta and tomato sauce. All varieties of the brand are low in fat, low in sugar and free from preservatives, added colours and flavours.

Heinz Spaghetti and Hoops have traditionally appealed to both children and their parents. Meal times are made fun as kids are inspired to create shapes, stories and landscapes. Without Heinz Spaghetti a sausage could never be an enemy submarine and the white cliffs would just be a wall of mashed potato! While kids find them fun to eat, mums are reassured that although the brand is healthy and nutritious, it is also quick, convenient and easy to prepare at mealtimes. The brand exemplifies Heinz's commitment to producing nutritious, high quality, family food with salt, sugar and fat content that meet the dietary standards of the Food Standards Agency and the Department of Health.

In 2005, Heinz put its biggest investment for decades behind Spaghetti, with a brand new kids range, reduced salt and fun new packaging. This investment revitalised the existing Heinz Spaghetti and Heinz Hoops packaging, and brought back the classic Heinz Alphabetti Spaghetti. The product itself was also enhanced with the texture of

the spaghetti improved, as well as the taste and texture of the tomato sauce.

As part of the investment, Heinz also launched a new range of Spaghetti shapes in tomato sauce. Heinz Space Spaghetti, Heinz Spaghetti Head and Heinz Funky Fish are 33% lower in salt, made from multigrain pasta, and have the same taste, texture and tomato sauce that kids enjoy. Again, although mums are reassured that the new range is healthy and nutritious, it also highlights Heinz's drive to make meal times fun for kids. Heinz Space Spaghetti contains intergalactic shapes such as astronauts, shooting stars, planets, moon buggies and space rockets. Meanwhile, Heinz Spaghetti

Head is like Mr Potato Head in a can, with eyes, ears, noses and mouths, and Heinz Funky Fish allows kids to create an underwater world with angelfish, starfish, sea horses, lobsters and dolphins.

How was the brand developed?

Heinz Spaghetti was launched in 1926 in response to consumer demand for greater variety and convenience of food. It was initially introduced in the US and Canada before being imported across the Atlantic. Since then, Heinz Spaghetti has frequently been eaten by generations and is a brand firmly established as part of British everyday mealtimes.

In 1930, the brand was manufactured for the first time at the Harlesden site in North London. Over 20 years later, in 1953 Heinz Spaghetti Hoops was launched; this was followed by Heinz Ravioli in 1965.

Prior to the re-launch of Heinz Spaghetti, research showed that canned spaghetti was being bought less frequently. Mums were beginning to question its nutritional value and there were a number of competing faster meal alternatives for young families. However, Heinz has placed emphasis on the nutritional integrity of its products, including reducing the salt content. Since its re-launch Heinz Spaghetti is growing at 3% year-on-year (Source: 12 W/E January 28th 2006).

Where would you have seen the brand?

The new Heinz Spaghetti shapes and its revitalised core range are available in supermarkets and convenience stores. Indeed, the brand has 98% distribution across the UK retail market. Heinz is a market leader with a 70.2% market share in the UK canned pasta market, which is worth £13.07 million (Source: IRI W/E January 28th 2006).

Heinz has also campaigned to help reduce salt intake among consumers. In November 2005, Heinz Spaghetti was part of an FSA campaign to encourage consumers to 'check out their salt level'. Similarly, the pasta shapes' salt reduction has been praised by CASH (Consensus Action on Salt and Health), whose research suggests that Heinz pasta shapes contain less salt than their nearest branded competitor.

What does the brand promise you?

The Heinz brand makes a central promise to consumers that it will produce high quality, nutritious family food. Heinz has adopted strict guidelines for salt, sugar and fat that meet the dietary standards endorsed and promoted by the Food Standards Agency and the Department of Health.

This promise is reflected in Heinz Spaghetti and Hoops, which are made from fresh pasta and fortified with vitamins and iron. They also contain no artificial colours, preservatives or flavours.

Heinz Spaghetti makes a dual promise: it brings fun to kids and reassurance to mums that the brand is nutritious as well as convenient. As its strap line states: 'Heinz Spaghetti – fun fuel for your kids' fun-filled days.'

Did you know?

Today over 103 million cans of Heinz Spaghetti and Heinz Spaghetti Hoops are sold each year in the UK. Meanwhile, hundreds of thousands more cans are exported around the world to homesick Brits who miss the Heinz taste.

Heinz Spaghetti is made from freshly made spaghetti. Pasta makers snip the freshly made spaghetti directly into the can moments before being topped up with a rich, tomato sauce and sealed tight to keep fresh.

Tinned Spaghetti is the fourth most commonly consumed kids' food, just below pizza (Source: FFP).

Each tin of Heinz Spaghetti contains 47% tomatoes.

Junior

Junior is a family lifestyle magazine targeted at a new generation of stylish parents, who are educated, discerning and driving trends for child-specific brands. Junior is a distinctive, glossy monthly title offering contemporary parenting and child-focused features balanced with luxurious children's fashion, inspired interiors, and luxury travel. It is a confident, intelligent read for the informed and involved modern parent.

What is Junior?

Junior is a well respected magazine brand with a distinctive presence in the parenting magazine market. It understands that the modern woman's desire for style, fashion, inspirational ideas, as well as intelligent debate and information, does not diminish with the onset of parenthood. The magazine celebrates children and family life throughout the magazine.

Working with talented photographers, designers and brands Junior uses stunning imagery to depict children's fashion and style ideas. For example, articles include features such as Philippe Starck discussing family-orientated interiors, alongside debate and expert opinion from Penelope Leach and Gina Ford, sitting among the new season's children's fashion from Ralph Lauren, Dior and Dolce & Gabbana.

The advertising in the magazine is predominantly luxury brands from fashion, interiors, and travel providing an additional source of inspiration to the readership. A large classified section also provides an arena for artisan companies offering bespoke children's products.

In acknowledgement of its strength within the London market, Junior has a dedicated London section focusing on family life in the capital – choices of areas to live; restaurants offering gourmet food in a family-friendly environment; educational highlights; the latest galleries and museum activities, as well as entertainment for children, are all covered.

Where would you have seen the brand?

The core business of the Junior brand is the magazine, which is sold through high street shops, supermarkets, and fashion boutiques. The title has a strong subscriptions base with around 40% of its sales. The magazine is also sold in around 20 countries around the world, which includes the recent launch of an Australian edition. Junior's sister title Junior Pregnancy & Baby is also widely available, which talks in the same way to expectant mothers. Both

titles have a strong web presence through the websites www.juniormagazine.co.uk and the associated fashion trade site www.juniorfashion.co.uk.

How was the brand developed?

The magazine was launched in December 1997 inspired by significant demographic and cultural changes across the UK, which had affected attitudes to parenting. A key trend had been the rise in age of first-time mothers, a trend predominantly driven by professional educated women delaying family life until career and personal ambitions have been satisfied.

At this time, Chris Taggart, the founder of Beach Magazines identified the lack of a title addressing the needs and desires of the professional, highly educated, stylish parent. He recognised the emergence of an educated, discerning, informed, concerned, demanding and fashionable

audience who were driving the desire and trends for child-specific brands from designer interiors and clothing, to organic foods and family oriented travel systems.

This trend is reflected in new children's brands from Dior children's boutique clothing to Zara's high street range; healthy ready supermarket meals for children; home furnishings from Designer's Guild to Next; child-focused designs in cars such as the Chrysler Voyager; and development of luxury child-friendly holidays from the Caribbean to skiing in the Alps.

The magazine's title 'Junior' was chosen as a name which would work internationally. Beach Magazines was bought by Future plc in January 2005 but Chris Taggart remains a consultant. Recent developments have included the launch of an Australian edition, and the further development of the website; other international editions are planned over the next two years.

What does the brand promise you?

Junior is passionate about children. It pledges to talk with readers in the same way as a friend would. Junior defines how the reader feels on their great days with its shared experience and celebration of parenthood – reflecting enjoyment, concern, information and advice. It acknowledges and reaffirms the reader as an involved and proactive parent who wants the best for their child and family, who is intelligent and informed.

It makes the reader feel confident and up-to-date. It empowers the reader through insight, reassurance, and choice. It is honest, expert, confident, as well as being stylish and idiosyncratic. Junior chooses never to criticise – instead it confidently asserts and presents the finest products and services selected by the magazine. Junior chooses never to offer opinion – its practice is to present the latest information, advice, or balance of expert view and anticipate that the reader will take their own path.

Did you know?

Junior's typical reader is a 35 year-old married woman with two pre-school children.

Average household income for readers of the title is over twice the national average of £26,000. Indeed, 20% have a household income in excess of £100,000.

A total of 40% of Junior's readers commit to buying the magazine regularly through subscription.

Other titles Junior's readers may read include Vogue, Red, Tatler, Good Housekeeping, Saturday Telegraph and The Sunday Times.

Kellogg's Coco Pops is a breakfast cereal for kids positioned around the idea of 'chocolatey' fun. It is targeted towards kids aged 6-8 years-old. The brand is about bringing fun to breakfast time, delivered by the way Coco Pops turns the milk 'chocolatey' and through the engaging advertising adventures of Coco the Monkey.

What is Coco Pops?

Coco Pops is made from puffed and toasted grains of rice, covered in a chocolate coating and fortified with calcium, iron and six vitamins. The children's breakfast cereal is widely recognised through the icon Coco the Monkey, who appears on the packaging and advertising. The brand, which is nearly 50 years-old, is also well-known for its famous advertising strap line: 'I'd rather have a bowl of Coco Pops.'

Where would you have seen the brand?

Coco Pops' main channel for its advertising is on kids TV and cinema with ads starring Coco the Monkey and his gang, battling against their adversary Crafty Croc to prevent him from getting his claws on their 'deliciously chocolatey' Coco Pops. Coco the Monkey and his jungle gang have been featuring in the iconic marketing since the brand was first advertised on TV over 20 years ago.

The brand also advertises across other media. A key part of its promotion comes from its website (www.cocopops.co.uk). The children's community website is themed around Coco's island and has a number of online team games for kids to play to win prizes, such as tickets to Alton Towers.

Sponsorship has also been used to drive brand awareness and endorsement.

Most recently Coco Pops Straws, the newest innovation from the brand, has begun sponsoring Saturday morning programming on Cartoon Network called 'Saturday Jungle'.

Coco Pops is available in supermarkets and most convenience stores. Its distinctive bright yellow packaging always features Coco the Monkey. Promotions on the pack play a key role in marketing, providing fun in and on the box. This ranges from associations with licences such as the Star Wars film in May 2005, to equity promotions relating to the Coco Pops storyline so kids can get involved in Coco's adventures.

How was the brand developed?

Coco Pops was launched by Kellogg's in 1960. Since then the brand has grown by 21% and is now worth £44.4 million (Source: IR). Innovation has played a crucial role in the brand's growth.

In 2001, the brand was first extended with Caramel Coco Pops, which was followed by Coco Pops Crunchers the following year. In 2004, the brand launched Coco Rocks, a breakfast cereal containing a mix of 'chocolatey rocks' – one crunchy rock, and the other with a smooth chocolate paste centre. Coco Rocks was the best performing cereal innovation of 2005 and grew to a value of £5 million just 10 months from launch (Source: IR).

Its newest innovation Coco Pops Straws has also been performing well since its launch in September 2005. It is an innovative new format for the breakfast cereal market – hollow tubes of cereal with a chocolate lining. It enables kids to suck their milk through the chocolate straws before eating them. The new product is being promoted through two adverts, one targeted to kids and one to their parents, a dual marketing approach which is a first for Coco Pops. The ad for parents demonstrates how Coco Pops Straws are a fun way to encourage kids to drink milk.

Coco Pops' iconic advertising has also evolved during the brand's 50 year history. In 1998, the brand changed its name from Coco Pops to Choco Krispies to pull the brand under one global umbrella. However, the move was unpopular with UK consumers. The following year, the brand used a TV ad to ask kids to vote on the name change. Most kids preferred the name Coco Pops so the brand was changed back.

The success of this interactive TV ad made the brand realise that its young consumers liked getting involved and this insight has shaped marketing campaigns ever since. Kids are now being asked to join in the fun by working out how Coco and his gang can get out of predicaments to save their beloved Coco Pops.

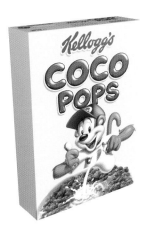

What does the brand promise you?

Coco Pops promises kids chocolatey fun. Through allowing kids to engage with and join in the adventures of Coco the Monkey and the gang, the brand offers children a sense of belonging. This is known to be one of the key emotions that motivates children alongside play, success and power.

Did you know?

Coco the Monkey has starred on Coco Pops' TV advertising for over 20 years.

Coco Pops is a global brand but is only called Coco Pops in the UK, and Choco Krispies in many countries across the rest of the world.

Sports presenter Des Lynam starred in a Coco Pops advert as a cartoon lion during its Jungle World Cup.

Coco the Monkey's gang include Shortie the Giraffe, Heftie the Hippo, Osmelda the Ostrich and Kylie the Kangeroo. The baddies include Crafty Croc and the two Gorilla Goons.

little tikes®

toys that last®

Little Tikes is renowned for its strong robust colourful toys for young children. The best known products are big, plastic toys such as the popular Cozy Coupe, a red and yellow play car which kids can propel with their feet. Little Tikes has been making active toys for kids since 1969 and believes that kids will always want to play imaginatively and climb and ride on toys.

What is Little Tikes?

Little Tikes has been described in the press as the purveyor of 'Big Plastic Playthings that are built to last' and is famous for its playhouses, climbers, kitchens and ride-on toys. The core audience for Little Tikes' products are pre-school children aged 0-5 years.

Little Tikes designs and develops high quality toys to encourage children to be active and to stimulate their imagination. The durability of Little Tikes' toys is reflected in its strap line – Toys That Last.

Products are available in a wide variety of categories for young children, including infant toys, popular sports, play trucks, ride-on toys, sandboxes, activity gyms and climbers, slides, pre-school development, role-play toys, creative arts and juvenile furniture.

The iconic Cozy Coupe car has sold over 200 million cars since its launch in the early 1970s and has retained popularity among kids despite being over 30 years old. Other popular Little Tikes' products include the Turtle Sandbox, Playground, Little Tikes Playhouse, The Whale Teeter Totter, the Large Car Transporter and the Easy Store Basketball set.

In order to stay ahead in the toy industry, Little Tikes tries to be innovative by developing several toys in one, such as the award-winning 5in1 Activity Gym, a toy for new born babies which is designed to grow with the child and adapts into a play table, a desk or an easel. It also develops a strong range of infant and pre-school toys such as the Handle Haulers – first trucks for toddlers.

Similarly, the Tikes Town Playhouse allows parents to interact with children. It is more than a playhouse as it provides four role play activities: a schoolhouse with chalkboard, a shop with a bank, a sports wall with basketball and football nets, and a petrol station.

Where would you have seen the brand?

The popularity of Little Tikes' products means that PR-related activity and product placement is effective. The company makes its products available at public events such as the Festival of Speed at Goodwood or in play areas at shopping centres and holiday resorts. Little Tikes is also a garden staple in many TV programmes on BBC and ITV.

In the UK, a number of PR initiatives have been pioneered. Little Tikes partnered with the Metropolitan Police to donate Cozy Coupe 'police cars' to pre-schoolers in the community to foster good relations with the police. The initiative inspired extensive press coverage.

In a similar community initiative, Little Tikes donated ride-on cars to children's

wards in hospitals. The hospital scheme was launched at Hammersmith Hospital and has been rolled out across the rest of the UK, France and Germany. This PR-driven campaign featured on several TV news bulletins and in the national press.

Little Tikes also partners with other brands. It ran a joint marketing campaign in national daily newspapers featuring Little Tikes playhouses through estate agents. A co-promotion with SMA, the baby milk formula, which provided Little Tikes products on special offer, led to increased sales for SMA and the response to the on-pack offer was three times greater than anticipated. It has also run a co-promotion with Tesco breakfast cereals with an offer running across two million packs.

What does the brand promise you?

Little Tikes develops toys to encourage imaginative play, which stimulate kids. The company believes in creating toys that last, because it is the best way to provide value for parents. Its robust, durable products, which encourage active play, are not dictated by fads or trends. Because of the belief that active play is more rewarding than passive pastimes, Little Tikes makes toys for each stage of a child's development, providing play activities from first gyms to playhouses and climbers.

How was the brand developed?

In 1969, Thomas Murdough Jr. started developing toys using rotational moulding techniques inside a barn in Ohio, US. Until this point, the method of developing large plastic products was restricted to other industries. The technique was adopted to develop strong and durable playhouses, kitchens, wagons and children's furniture – and the brand was established. This method of production provides the inherent strength and durability, the double-wall thickness of the toys, upon which the reputation of the brand was founded.

Little Tikes grew quickly with its range of large 'roto-moulded' products which children could play on or in, rather than just with. It was bought by the giant Rubbermaid Organisation, who continued to develop the brand. The original belief continues to be that children will always want to climb and ride on toys, despite the lure of hi-tech playthings. However, the brand started to introduce electronic features to some toys allowing kids to 'discover' and develop their imagination through sound and light features as well.

Little Tikes was first introduced in the UK in the mid-1970s, and instantly appealed to parents who were looking for strong, good quality toys. It was introduced through nurseries where toys get a real hammering, and from there, to the toy specialists.

Sales grew dramatically with the introduction of Toys R Us to the UK, where large toys were able to be given display space in-store. The UK operation of Toys R Us is one of Little Tikes' top global retail customers.

Did you know?

If you stacked all the Cozy Coupes sold since its launch on top of each other they would be 11,270 miles high and reach far into space. The Cozy Coupe tower would be 43,103 times higher than the Empire State Building.

The Cozy Coupe is one of the best-selling cars in America and has sold over 20 million since launch.

For nearly 50 years, Matey bubble bath has been a firm family favourite. Since its launch in 1958, Matey has been the kids' number one bubble bath in the UK (Source: IRI). The total children's bath market is worth £4 million and Matey holds a 40% share (Source: IRI data 52 W/E January 22nd 2006) making it the number one children's bathing product. Its long history means that Matey is a nostalgic brand with many parents remembering the skittle-shaped bottles from their own childhood bath times. Today, despite kids growing up in a world of technology and gadgets, Matey remains popular because it goes back to basics and encourages imagination and fun.

What is Matey?

Matey bubble bath is available in four collectable bottles: Sailor Matey, Mer-Matey, Lucky Matey and Doc-topus Matey. Each product has a different colour formulation and a different fragrance.

Sailor Matey, who is the captain of HMS Matey, is the brand's biggest seller and has been the star of the Matey range since its launch nearly 50 years ago. Sailor Matey, which is a blue-coloured bubble bath, has an 18% share of the total kids bubble bath market (Source: IRI data 52 W/E January 2006).

Mer-Matey is a pink mermaid with golden hair. She began life years ago as Miss Matey, a female sailor, but has since transformed into a mermaid who playfully makes pink bubbles.

Lucky Matey is the green pirate parrot who produces green-coloured bubble bath.

Finally, the most recent variant of Matey, launched in 2000, is Doc-topus Matey, which has a colour-changing formulation. The bubble bath liquid is red in the bottle but changes to blue when mixed with water.

Children aged one and over are Matey's key users, because bath times are fun times. Toddlers and young children love splashing about in a bath full of bubbles and also enjoy playing with Matey's fun, bright, packaging.

Matey's washing and bathing products are also targeted to appeal to parents. The brand's gentle formulation ensures it can help to care for kids' skin and helps keep them clean, while the packs serve to entertain and engage them during bath time. All Matey products are dermatologically tested and approved. They are also pH balanced and contain added moisturisers. This means that the brand has occupied a unique position in the market being both fun for children, and also helping to care for skin which is reassuring to parents.

Where would you have seen the brand?

Matey is available from chemists and supermarkets. Currently, key brand communication is through PR strategies. For example, its characters appear in and support children's books. This strategy is demonstrated with the Chuckle book which is a free games book distributed in children's hospitals.

Today, the Matey website, www.matey.co.uk, plays an important role in boosting the brand's relationship with its young consumers. Set on the Matey Island it is filled with fun, interactive, educational games. For example, kids can click on the Matey mermaid to send an online postcard, or click through to the Matey Sailor to play a treasure trail game and visit the Matey starfish for its colouring pages.

In the past the Matey brand has been marketed through press and radio advertising. Its well-known advertising jingle from the 1960s and 1970s can be downloaded from the website and has become a classic: 'Your Matey's a bottle of fun, You puts me in the bath, I'm loved by everyone, I'm always good for a laugh.' Today Matey's strap line – 'Go Bubbleistic' – plays a central role in marketing.

What does the brand promise you?

Matey provides trusted bathtime fun for parents and their children. In a world of increasing technology and complexity, Matey offers back to basics, light hearted fun for kids.

How was the brand developed?

Matey was launched in 1958 with its original character Sailor Matey. The brand was developed in the 1960s with four variants: Matey, Miss Matey and then two seasonal ranges – Santa Matey and Rudolph Matey. The distinctive Matey cap, which sits like a hat on the brand's characters, was devised in the 1960s and is recognised today as a registered trademark.

In 1992, the brand was re-launched with the introduction of some new characters including Snowy Matey and Wizard Matey. Four years later, the brand was re-launched again and extended into a body wash, hand wash and shampoo. However, in 2000 the decision was made for the brand to refocus on its core variants of bubble bath and the current characters were introduced with the aim to maintain the range's famous nautical theme.

Did you know?

Matey is the original children's bubble bath.

Since its original launch, Sailor Matey, the hero of the range, has had 12 re-designs. He has been accompanied by 25 different friends since then including Wizard Matey and Santa Matey.

The distinctive bath cap was devised in the early 1960s and it is still registered today as a Matey trademark, symbolising bath time fun.

milkshake!

Milkshake! is a well-loved children's TV brand for 2-6 year-olds. Featured on Five, the British terrestrial channel, Milkshake! transmits every morning from 6am until 9am with high quality programmes that are entertaining, stimulating and educational. Among 4-6 year-olds, Milkshake! is the most popular pre-school programme strand, according to the latest BARB data.

What is Milkshake!?

Milkshake!'s safe, fun and imaginative programmes include animation, 'claymation', puppet and live action shows for its pre-school audience. Milkshake! combines new hits such as Fifi and the Flowertots and Peppa Pig, with classics such as Make Way for Noddy, and live action programmes such as Hi 5 and of course the Milkshake! presenters.

Naomi Wilkinson, Kemi Majeks and Beth Evans are the three wholesome, regular faces of Milkshake! loved by pre-schoolers across the country. With their own style of presenting each one starts the morning with a smile and a warm welcome, introducing all the Milkshake! shows. Crucial to the Milkshake! brand, the three presenters sing the soundtrack, and feature in the new title sequence of the programming strand.

As well as announcing some of the UK's best loved pre-school shows including Make Way For Noddy, Peppa Pig and Fifi and the Flowertots, the girls also read out birthday cards and messages to the young viewers. Hundreds of Milkshake! fans send in their best drawings for the presenters every week.

The Milkshake! presenters have also brought viewers closer to the brand's characters with interviews with Bear from Bear in the Big Blue House, Noddy and Winnie the Pooh.

Keen for its viewers to be healthy, happy and active, the Milkshake! presenters additionally encourage morning activity through the 'Milkshake! Shake', a special exercise for their young audience.

The Milkshake! team have also produced their own 10-part series with A Milkshake! Christmas and A Milkshake! Summer. Each 30 minute programme was filled with stories, songs and challenges, as well as things to make and do.

Milkshake! has been fortunate enough to have its characters brought to life by some very famous people. They include children's presenter Brian Cant, and actresses Miranda Richardson and Fiona Shaw. This year, comedian and TV presenter Julian Clary will be providing the voiceover for a new Milkshake! show – The Little Princess.

Milkshake!
Featuring Noddy and Peppa Pig
6am, 7 days a week

five

Where would you have seen the brand?

TV promotions on Five use the marketing tag line: 'For happy contented children give them Milkshake for breakfast.' The Milkshake! brand is also marketed through its website www.five.tv/milkshake. With around 575,000 page impressions and 56,000 visits a month, the Milkshake! website is one of the most popular areas of the Five portal. It was re-launched in September 2004 to make it more interactive and engaging for viewers enabling them to play with their favourite characters.

This year, the Milkshake! brand is going on tour to Butlins. Visiting Butlins' three holiday resorts in Bognor, Skegness and Minehead. The 57 date tour will be spread across 19 weeks between May and October with three live shows a week, featuring its favourite characters and the Milkshake! presenters.

Children will also be able to enjoy the Milkshake! experience beyond the regular TV strand, through a compilation DVD. The first DVD, Milkshake! Treats will launch this spring, featuring over 100 minutes of the viewer's favourite Milkshake! programmes Five is hoping that the Milkshake! compilation will become an annual release.

Five also plans to extend Milkshake! into a range of merchandise, following the August 2005 appointment of Target Licensing to manage the brand extension. The new Milkshake! range will initially focus on arts and crafts, clothing, cards, accessories, and a back-to-school collection with a launch date of 2007.

What does the brand promise you?

Milkshake!'s reliable and responsible schedule caters for pre-schoolers and their parents, reassuring families that this TV brand will look after your children. Milkshake! offers wholesome programming with a mixture of established and nostalgic programmes like Bagpuss, with newer launches such as Fifi and the Flowertots. It reinforces itself as a destination of safe television with characters that parents recognise and love from their own past.

Did you know?

Richard Briers is the voice behind Milkshake!'s shows Roobarb and Custard, and Roobarb and Custard Too.

Actress Jane Horrocks, best known for her starring role in the film, Little Voice and as Bubbles in Absolutely Fabulous, is also the voice behind Fifi and the Flowertots.

Mark Williams, the comedian from The Fast Show is the voice behind the Milkshake! programme Funky Valley.

Even classical actors and actresses feature on Milkshake! Fiona Shaw, best known for her Shakespearian and theatre performances is the voice behind Ebb and Flo.

Hugh Laurie, who was recently awarded a Golden Globe for his portrayal of a brilliant, but cynical doctor in Five's series House, also plays a starring role as the voice behind Milkshake!'s MechaNick.

How was the brand developed?

Since Five's launch in March 1997, as Channel Five, the terrestrial TV channel has always catered for children, under the direction of Nick Wilson, controller of children's programming. However, four years ago, Five decided to launch a special children's brand to pull its pre-school programming under one umbrella.

Wilson named the new brand Milkshake! because he wanted the programming strand to feel like a children's coffee morning. So while adults go to coffee mornings, children go to Milkshake!

Milkshake! launched with children's series such as Havakzoo and Beachcomber Bay. As the strand developed, acquisitions such as Bear in the Big Blue House were brought into the schedule to huge success. The brand grew from strength to strength as characters such as household names Winnie the Pooh and Noddy were introduced.

More recently, Five has secured the British broadcast rights for a new animated TV series called Rupert and Friends. Featuring Rupert Bear, the new show will appear on Milkshake! from autumn 2006. Other new highlights for 2006 include Say It With Noddy, Funky Town (a spin off of Funky Valley) and The Little Princess.

Mother &Baby

Mother & Baby is a brand that offers support and empathy for women facing the experiences of pregnancy, birth, new motherhood and raising children through its magazine, website, reader events and awards.

Mother & Baby combines modernity and up-to-date knowledge with the heritage of a 50 year-old brand. It demonstrates expertise of all baby products and is often a trusted guide for mothers before they make large purchases. In addition, the Mother & Baby Awards are a well respected stamp of approval.

What is Mother & Baby magazine?

Mother & Baby is the UK's number one parenting magazine (ABC J-D05). The brand is supported by a website and the Mother & Baby Awards which are now in their 14th year and are widely recognised as a reliable indicator of the best baby products. The British brand is known internationally and syndicated to six countries worldwide; meanwhile the UK magazine is sold in an additional 14 countries.

The magazine prides itself on providing must-read pregnancy, baby and toddler health information. It is also an expert on baby products, testing products on real mums, whose opinions are the most sought-after by readers.

The brand offers guidance and real-life advice to young mothers in an informative, fun and reassuring way. Mother & Baby is also a campaigning magazine that works hard to improve and change issues that its readers care about. To date the brand has campaigned on issues including car seat legislation, baby first aid, birth in the NHS and the pressures on young mums to be as skinny as post-birth celebrities.

Where would you have seen the brand?

Mother & Baby magazine is available on newsstands nationwide – from supermarkets to small independent newsagents across the UK. The brand's website www.motherandbabymagazine.com also plays a vital role in marketing the brand and providing information to its audience. The website has an incredibly active community of mums providing them with a large variety of content and interactive features.

Similarly, the Mother & Baby Awards is a high profile event and boosts awareness of the brand. The event logo is frequently used by award-winning brands in advertising and on product packaging.

The Mother & Baby brand is additionally promoted through its role as a campaigner. Its editor, Elena Dalrymple, often acts as a spokesperson for mums and parents, appearing on TV news programmes and chat shows, on national and regional radio, as well as in national and regional newspapers and other magazines.

The brand has also won some awards of its own. In 2004, the Mother & Baby Save A Life Campaign, in association with Tesco, won The Grocer Award for Best

Campaign. The brand also won Magazine of the Year at the Emap Communications Award 2003.

How was the brand developed?

Mother & Baby launched in 1956 and the brand has been informing, entertaining and reassuring mums for 50 years. Although society has changed, mums in 2006 have similar parenting concerns as their grandmothers did in 1956.

Is their baby developing normally? What should they do when illness strikes? Which product is best for them and their baby? How will a baby change their relationship with their partner? And could their baby be put on the cover of Mother & Baby? These are all issues that are as relevant today as they were when the magazine launched 50 years ago.

The Mother & Baby Awards launched in 1993 and are now entering their 14th successful year to become one of the highlights of the nursery industry calendar. When the awards were first launched the

What does the brand promise you?

Mother & Baby's brand values are celebratory, real and reassuring. The magazine is all-inclusive and wants to speak to all mums, regardless of age, cultural background or economic circumstances, about the challenges and opportunities that they face.

The brand champions the rights of mums today and believes that every mother knows what's best for her baby, family and herself. The brand aims to give mums confidence to make informed choices for their baby.

lunchtime ceremony was attended by 50 clients. Today the annual evening event is attended by 650 people.

When it first launched there were only 11 category winners, this has grown to 30. In 2005 over 413 products were entered and 153 products made it through to the short-list. All the short-listed products go through a vigorous testing process which is judged on quality, innovation, design, value for money, unique selling points, price and packaging. This testing process takes over six weeks and products are tested by over 350 mums.

The Mother & Baby brand is also proud of its campaigning side. As well as running award-winning first aid courses it has raised public awareness around serious issues facing mums today such as the struggle to balance work and motherhood, the cost of childcare and the brutality of giving birth in the NHS system. Since 1998, the brand has campaigned for a change in car seat legislation to better protect children travelling in cars. This is due to come into effect later this year.

Mother & Baby magazine launched its website in January 2005 and it already features a busy online community. The website partners the magazine and covers all areas to do with having a baby from conception, through to pregnancy and birth, from how to deal with a newborn right through to toddler-related issues.

Did you know?

The first editor of Mother & Baby was one of 16 children.

Steps, the charity for children with lower-limb conditions, was set up in 1980 after a Mother & Baby reader wrote to the magazine about her baby, who was born with club foot. She received so many letters in response that she formed a national support group.

The Mother & Baby Save A Life courses have trained over 3,500 parents in baby first aid.

Mother & Baby magazine is 50 years-old in 2006.

605,000 pregnant women and mothers read Mother & Baby magazine every month.

Mountain Buggy is a strong, durable, robust brand for families who want the freedom of an outdoor lifestyle. Its range of all-terrain three and four wheeler buggies provide a choice of child transport suitable for either country or urban activity.

What is Mountain Buggy?

The core product of the Mountain Buggy brand is a rugged, three-wheeler pushchair that can ride over bumpier outdoor surfaces as well as city pavements. The easy-to-fold pushchair is suitable for children from newborns to four years-old. It can also be converted from a pushchair into a pram or child car seat carrier. The Mountain Buggy brand is available in three different product ranges: Urban, Terrain and Breeze.

The Mountain Buggy Terrain is the benchmark buggy which has built the Mountain Buggy's reputation. A true off-road buggy, it has been made for running, mountain walks, the beach, gravel roads and the farm, but can still be used in the city. Excellent balancing means it is easy to tilt and turn and it features simplicity, strength, safety and ease of use. The fixed front wheel is well-suited for uneven ground as there is no need for constant steering. A double Terrain is also available.

The Mountain Buggy Urban is for city parents who want the best of both worlds. While they may not utilise the strength and off-road capabilities they still want the safety, comfort and look of a rugged design. The Urban's 'lockable' swivel front wheel makes it easy to manoeuvre around

busy streets or use for the occasional foray onto rough terrain. It is also available as a double or triple buggy.

The Breeze Mountain Buggy model is smaller, lighter and more compact for young families who live in cities. It is ideally designed for crowded spaces, smaller cars and city living. It is suitable for newborns to children aged three years-old.

Mountain Buggy provides a number of accessories for its products such as a sleeping bag, a storm cover and UV sun cover. Other accessories available include a hand brake for the Terrain, a nappy changing bag and a travel bag to protect the brand on trips.

The Mountain Buggy carrycot can be slotted into the pushchair's frame to make a pram for younger babies or the car seat clip can be attached to enable use of a car seat. Mountain Buggy has adapted its models to be compatible with Lascal's Kiddyboard and Buggyboard. It is one of the few pushchair brands that enables an additional child to be carried on the boards without invalidating the warranty.

How was the brand developed?

The original Mountain Buggy was born in 1992, in the Croad family garage in New Zealand. It consisted of a car seat attached by bungee cords to an old golf trundler purchased for NZ$5 at a school gala.

Where would you have seen the brand?

Mountain Buggy's product range is stocked in leading independent specialist shops as well as department stores on the high street such as John Lewis. The brand's awareness is boosted through a variety of different media channels from consumer exhibitions such as The Baby Show to classified ads and product tests in the parenting press.

Over the years Mountain Buggy has consistently achieved awards such as Editor's Choice in Practical Parenting in 2004 and Junior Magazine in 2004, Gold and Silver Awards in Baby & Toddler Gear in 2004 and 2005, and Mumsnet Best Choice in 2005 and 2006. Similarly, Mountain Buggy has been recommended by leading consumer test magazines in the UK and abroad.

NEW ZEALAND MADE

Allan Croad's Mountain Buggy grew from the desire to have a sturdy practical baby buggy that would allow him and wife Adrienne to continue their active outdoor lifestyle.

A further development of this prototype was used by Allan to run a half marathon – it worked well and he was approached by a small number of runners and spectators who could see the merits of using a buggy themselves. A few tweaks here and there and the Mountain Buggy brand had arrived.

The Mountain Buggy has grown to be a market leader in its home market of New Zealand. In 1995 the first Mountain Buggies were exported to the UK and set a precedent for simple, innovative and sturdy child transport design. The brand is now sold in over 20 countries around the world including the US, Canada and Europe.

What does the brand promise you?

Mountain Buggy is a robust, easy-to-use, safe and premium brand for parents who want to share their passion of the great outdoors with their young children. It's a brand that represents freedom because it enables families to continue to enjoy outdoor activities without restrictions. Mountain Buggy is a customer-focused brand that listens to its consumers. Ongoing improvements are inspired by suggestions from parents who use its products.

Did you know?

It took 10 months to sell the first 10 Mountain Buggies in the UK – 10 years later the niche market product sells 5,000 annually and is still growing.

Mountain Buggy is a popular brand with celebrities – one famous family own five.

Mountain Buggy made a guest appearance in an episode of comedy TV series Absolutely Fabulous as well as in an article in Time magazine.

www.muller.co.uk

Müller provides consumers with a range of different yogurts, yogurt drinks and desserts. Using the strap line 'Lead a Müller Life', the brand places emphasis on enjoying life and being healthy. Müller's range provides a wide variety of products for a broad spectrum of consumers.

What is Müller?

Müller provides a wide range of products and snacks that cover both the healthy eating and indulgent markets. Müller is the market leader in the Short Life Dairy Products (SLDP) category.

There are a number of different products among the range, which appeal to children aged five and over, especially the Müller Corner and Müller Vitality brands. The 'split' concept of Müller Corner, which provides yogurt with a separate portion of fruit or crunchy cereal, creates a tangible interest for kids.

Similarly, the pre and probiotic range of Müller Vitality yogurts and yogurt drinks have proved popular among families. They are helping to address increasing concerns over children's health, while the handy drink format of Müller Vitality appeals to all the family.

The Müller Vitality range is the second largest brand within the drinking yogurt sector with an 11.1% value share of the £267 million market. This market is constantly growing and evolving, which means Müller Vitality must continually innovate and develop new products.

Müller Corner is the number one yogurt brand in the UK. Its key proposition is, 'something for everyone', which is represented in the 21 different flavours it offers. Müller Corner's concept of offering yogurt with a separate portion can appeal to all ages. Innovative flavours such as the Crunch varieties, which combine vanilla yogurt with chocolate balls, or yogurt with toffee hoops, for example, are especially popular among children. Müller Corner also offers a snack-size product, ideal for lunchboxes, available in strawberry, the consumer's favourite flavour.

In 2005, Müller Corner's Healthy Balance range was introduced to extend the brand portfolio and ensure the Corner range was catering for both the indulgent and health markets. The Healthy Balance range features probiotic yogurt and low fat fruity and crunch portions in a variety of flavours.

Müller Corner also launched a range of American Classic desserts in July 2005. There are four different flavours: Alabama Chocolate Fudge Cake, Blueberry Manhattan Cheesecake, Florida Key Lime Pie and New England Banoffee Pie.

Where would you have seen the brand?

The brand's strap line, 'Lead a Müller Life', forms the central message for the company's umbrella marketing campaign. All marketing activity from Müller, while targeting various segments for each brand, aims to appeal to a wide audience by communicating different choices for all the family.

A high profile TV advertising campaign ran throughout 2005 focusing on 'Lead a Müller Life'. It starred a memorable song by Nina Simone, called 'Ain't Got No - I Got Life'. The track has since been released on the new compilation album 'We Love Life'.

Müller uses high profile PR to raise awareness of the brand. Sponsorship of high profile TV programmes is also planned for 2006.

Additionally, in-store promotion and nationwide sampling are important tools for generating trial of all Müller products. The brand has significant presence in the chiller cabinet across all supermarkets, as well as independent retailers.

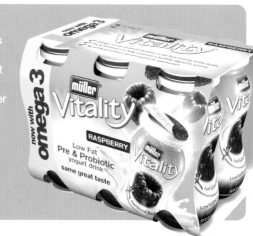

What does the brand promise you?

Müller's brand is centred on its strap line, 'Lead a Müller Life.' It's an inclusive, feel-good brand, where community is important.

How was the brand developed?

Müller was established in 1896 by Ludwig Müller, grandfather of the present owner, in a small Bavarian dairy. Today, the founder's grandson Theo runs a business with a 2.5 billion euro turnover and 5,244 employees.

Theo Müller took control of the company in 1970 and recognised the opportunity to expand the products from small, popular, regional brands to those with nationwide appeal, by improving the recipes. With this principle in place, the company began to grow very quickly.

In 1980 Müller launched an innovative product which had both fruit sauce and dairy rice in the same container; it proved so popular that Müllerice was later launched nationally. The innovation continued with the launch of Müller Corner into the UK in 1987 using the now well loved split pot. The Müllerlight range then followed, offering UK

consumers a large range of flavours of virtually fat-free yogurts.

The pace of the UK company's growth was swift and in 1991 construction started on a state of the art production facility in Market Drayton, Shropshire. In 1992 Müller achieved the coveted status of market leader. It had taken the brand just five years to climb to the top of the British market.

Since 2000, the brand has continued to expand and innovate with the launch of the Müller Vitality range, taking Müller into the probiotic market with its feel good bacteria. In light of the success of this market, Müller recently added probiotic good bacteria to the Müllerlight range and the Healthy Balance range from Müller Corner. Müller Vitality has also recently been re-launched with Omega-3 essential fatty acids.

Did you know?

Every week over 35 million pots leave the Müller factory in Market Drayton. That's three million pots a day, 125,000 an hour or 2,000 every minute.

700,000 litres of milk are delivered to the Market Drayton site every day from local suppliers.

Müller has a range of over 70 different yogurts and desserts.

The Müller factory has one of Europe's largest fruit plants, capable of cooking up to 140 tonnes of fruit every day.

From shark-infested custard, to cows jumping over the moon or Little Miss Muffet eating her curds and whey, the dairy world has always fuelled the imaginations, as well as the appetites of kids. And this is something that the Munch Bunch brand never forgets, because growing up is as much about developing creativity as it is about developing strong bones and bodies.

Munch Bunch provides kids with tasty yogurts that contain the nutritious benefits of protein and calcium, but also come with large helpings of fun. It's a combination that makes Munch Bunch 'great for growing kids™'.

What is Munch Bunch?

Munch Bunch is a range of fromage frais, wholemilk yogurts and drinking yogurts that are designed especially for kids. A child's healthy development is often down to what they eat on a day-to-day basis, which is why Nestlé has created a range of products to help kids eat healthily throughout the day, every day.

Nestlé's drive to develop healthier snacks for children to eat or drink throughout the day means that it's no longer just wholemilk yogurts and fromage frais that Munch Bunch is famed for. Nestlé has a complete range of healthier and fun products designed specifically for growing kids.

Munch Bunch Drinky+ is a probiotic drinking yogurt to help give kids a healthier start in the mornings. It contains a child-friendly probiotic 'Lactobacillus Fortis' to help keep little tummies healthy. This product is unique to Nestlé and the probiotic is especially designed for children. Munch Bunch Drinky+ now also contains Omega-3.

Meanwhile, Munch Bunch Mega Drinky is a drinking yogurt designed to be consumed after school, while the Munch Bunch Mega Double Up Fromage Frais is a fun twin-layered snack. Munch Bunch Fromage Frais is also available in two different sizes – a 42g pot for those with little appetites and an 80g pot for older, hungrier kids.

All Munch Bunch products are designed with the needs of growing kids in mind – the 'Munch Bunch Growth Formula' that appears on all products, for example, tells parents how much calcium each product provides, and also guarantees the use of real fruit purée and no artificial colouring. Just two small pots of Fromage Frais, for example, contain the same amount of calcium that is found in a 100ml glass of milk.

Where would you have seen the brand?

Since Nestlé acquired the brand four years ago, Munch Bunch's positioning has been clarified and reinforced. In a market where competitors are either focused exclusively on either health or fun, Munch Bunch strives to make healthier food fun. The resulting 'Through the legs' advert became the most successful Munch Bunch TV spot under Nestlé.

The ad was a success as it not only spoke to mums about the clear benefits of the product to their children but did so in an amusing and fun way that brought a

150ml glass

smile to the face of both mums and kids. 'Through the legs' was short-listed for a Cannes Lion award in 2004.

How was the brand developed?

The Munch Bunch was the creation of the imagination of a 14 year-old teenager called Angela Mitford. She drew the original illustrations in the late 1970s. Studio Publications then created a set of books, one for each of the 26 fruit and vegetable characters.

The Munch Bunch was a pile of unwanted fruit, vegetables and nuts, swept away in the corner of the greengrocer's

What does the brand promise you?

A good diet is essential for healthy development, but Munch Bunch believes that healthier eating shouldn't be about boring routines. As every parent knows, you can't spoon-feed kids forever, even when it comes to yogurt. Children need to discover things for themselves – which is why the Munch Bunch brand is committed to helping kids develop good eating habits all by themselves.

By making food both tasty and fun, Munch Bunch aims to make healthier eating an enjoyable and pleasurable experience for kids. Healthy eating should be something which kids will actively and independently seek out in the future. Munch Bunch is committed to making it a fun habit that kids want to pick up.

shop... until one very special night when, one by one, they came to life. The Munch Bunch included Sally Strawberry, Emma Apple, Lucy Lemon, Pippa Pear, Tom Tomato and Rozzy Raspberry as well as their less famous friends Barnabus Beetroot, Supercool Cucumber and Rory Rhubarb.

The group's adventures began when Spud, their leader, organised an escape from the grocer's shop to the bottom of the garden, where they decided to live in and around an old deserted garden shed. Due to their massive popularity a Munch Bunch TV show was created and 52 episodes were made and shown on TV between 1978 and 1980.

In the early 1980s Eden Vale acquired the food licence for the Munch Bunch and

quickly launched four single pot yogurts. By this point the Munch Bunch was no longer simply a book series and a TV show. It had also grown to include the infamous 'Munch Bunch Club', a newsletter providing activities to keep kids entertained.

In the mid 1980s, Munch Bunch's owner, Studio Publications, was taken over by Ladybird Books. Then a few years later, Eden Vale bought the Munch Bunch property from them. In 1991, Northern Foods acquired Eden Vale and took over the Munch Bunch yogurts. Nestlé then acquired the Munch Bunch brand in 2002. Since then, Nestlé has focused on making fun healthy again, rejuvenating the core values that Munch Bunch stood for, for over two decades.

Did you know?

Each year the weight of Munch Bunch produced is equivalent to 3,500 elephants. Try carrying that in your lunch box.

The total amount of Munch Bunch consumed in 2005 was enough to fill over 30 Olympic-sized swimming pools.

If you lined up, end to end, all the Munch Bunch six-pack Fromage Frais sold in a year, you would be able to travel from Lands End to John o'Groats AND back again.

NIVEA Sun offers a full range of sun care products from lotions, sprays and after sun, to dedicated children's and baby's products. The brand combines the care promised by NIVEA with effective sun protection for families.

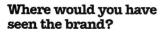

What is NIVEA Sun?

NIVEA Sun offers sun care products for the whole family. The core range includes NIVEA Sun Moisturising Sun Lotions and Moisturising Sun Sprays in a variety of sun protection factors (SPFs) to suit varying personal requirements such as skin type, age and holiday destination. The spectrum of protection spans from SPF 4 to SPF 50+.

The NIVEA Sun range includes After Sun, which is specially formulated to cool and soothe the skin after it has been exposed to the sun. It also helps maintain a tan for longer. Additionally, NIVEA Sun has a range of self tanning products. These include self tan wipes, aerosol sprays, lotions, face creams and pump spray.

The NIVEA Sun children's range comes in both lotions and sprays. The sprays are lightly-coloured to help application and make sun protection more fun for kids. The newest addition to the range is the NIVEA Sun Baby Sun Lotion SPF 50+. This lotion is specially formulated to suit delicate baby's skin and is enriched with moisturiser.

NIVEA Sun advises against babies being exposed to direct sunlight. This product is ideal for protection from reflected sunlight.

How was the brand developed?

The history of NIVEA Sun products can be traced back to 1934 when NIVEA Nut Oil was launched. This was followed 20 years later with the launch of Ultra Oil and Ultra Oil Spray. In 1960, NIVEA Sun was launched into the UK and 10 years later NIVEA Sun products were advertised in their own right.

In 1990, the brand's owner, Beiersdorf, introduced a completely revamped NIVEA Sun programme. This saw the range launched as a sub brand, with the word 'sun' translated into the language of each respective country in which it was launched. Three years later, the brand was globally aligned and NIVEA Sun was adopted as an international brand name.

1997 saw the brand launch its first sun products specifically created for kids called NIVEA Children Sun Protection. NIVEA Sun continued to add innovations to its portfolio with the introduction of Sun Spray in 1999, Firming Sun Lotion in 2002 and Moisturising Sun Lotion and Sprays with immediate protection in 2005.

This year, the NIVEA Sun's children range has been re-launched. All of the lotions and sprays now offer immediate protection and long-lasting water resistance. NIVEA Sun's emphasis on innovation means the brand can claim a number of firsts in the sun care protection market. It was the first to launch products with immediate protection and also the first to create SPF 50+ sprays both for adults and children.

Where would you have seen the brand?

NIVEA Sun® is available on the high street and found in all major UK retailers including Boots, Superdrug, Tesco, Sainsbury's and ASDA. Despite the cluttered market, the brand uses creativity and a strong, educational message to stand out from the crowd.

Its point of sale material in retail outlets includes educational information about sun protection. Also, NIVEA Sun's links with the Rapport Group (an organisation which links young people and brands) to provide teaching materials for primary schools, emphasises its commitment to education. The NIVEA Sun learning resources help teachers communicate the importance of sun care protection to young children. Additionally, the brand's sponsorship of the Tussauds theme park reinforces the importance of sun protection, even on a day out in the UK.

NIVEA Sun's successful marketing campaign has propelled NIVEA Sun Children Protection to become the leader of its category with a 45% market share in value (Source: IRI 52 W/E December 24th 2005). NIVEA Sun total market share is

17.5% in the sun preparations category (Source: IRI 52 W/E December 24th 2005).

In 2005 NIVEA Sun also won a number of awards. They include the Cosmopolitan Beauty Award with NIVEA Sun Moisturising Sun Lotion SPF 15 winning the Best SPF for the Body; while NIVEA Sun Moisturising Lotion and Spray won Best Sun Care Launch in the Pure Beauty Awards.

What does the brand promise you?

NIVEA Sun is committed to ensuring its consumers are safer in the sun. Its children's range reassures parents that their kids are well-protected while enjoying the sunshine. NIVEA's commitment to safety in the sun is emphasised by the brand's involvement in sun protection education as well as its continual new product development, which ensures consumers are protected as much as possible. NIVEA's desire to exceed consumer expectations leads it to develop new products every year.

Did you know?

The UK is the biggest country in terms of NIVEA Sun sales in the whole of the Beiersdorf world.

NIVEA products are used by half a billion people worldwide and 18 million products are sold per year.

In 2006, Beiersdorf, NIVEA's owner, will celebrate its UK centenary.

PEZ dispensers, the toy, sweet and collectable in one, have become a global household name. For decades, many famous comic and cartoon characters have been transformed into PEZ dispensers.

A constant stream of new and varied character heads keep the brand fresh. According to Big Kick Research in the UK, the brand is widely known among 6-10 year-olds and most children in this age group have at least one dispenser. In addition, many 9-10 year-olds also collect PEZ dispensers.

What is PEZ?

There are a lot of sweet dispensers on the market but only PEZ has the classic patented dispenser and the latest character heads. Consumers easily recognise the genuine article.

The compressed PEZ sweets are tablet-shaped to ensure they fit snugly into the dispenser. Single sweets can be dispensed through lifting the dispensers head. They are available in strawberry, lemon, orange and cherry flavours. All PEZ sweets are made without colourings, which mean they do not contain any E numbers.

PEZ dispensers span a broad product range inspired by the top licensing themes from the world of cartoon and comic heroes. Classic licenses include The Jungle Book, Winnie the Pooh, Mickey Mouse, The Lion King and Looney Tunes. PEZ also recreates top characters from the latest films such as Madagascar, Star Wars and Shrek, which have a relatively short life-cycle compared to the iconic dispensers.

The product range also includes numerous in-house creations as well as seasonal products. These include the 30cm tall XXL PEZ dispenser, the PEZ Racing Car dispenser and Mini Fantastic PEZ dispensers in the form of little fluffy animals.

As well as being popular with children, PEZ has become a cool collectable amongst adults. Collectors are known to be in continuous contact with each other around the globe, in order to extend their collections. Similarly, PEZ is becoming increasingly popular with students and young adults, who view the PEZ dispenser as a cult object and fashion accessory.

Where would you have seen the brand?

PEZ dispensers and refills are readily available on the high street. They are sold in supermarkets, selected independent newsagents and corner shops as well as some department stores and high street fashion stores.

PEZ licenses change every two months to keep up with the latest cartoon and comic characters and to retain the interest of children and collectors. These constant changes help to strengthen and revive the brand and ensure PEZ remains relevant to its young audience.

PEZ has a strong and colourful marketing history, with advertising dating back to the 1920s, which focused on the brand's benefits and values. In 2002 and 2003 PEZ

launched TV advertising which boosted its brand awareness immensely. Since then, PEZ has focused on integrated campaigns which include online marketing, sampling, PR, direct marketing and ambient media.

The central message of the brand's current campaign is: 'PEZ – the coolest collectable on the planet.' PEZ offers a

sweet, toy and collectable in one, so therefore has three different target groups it needs to consider in its marketing: children, which are the largest audience, followed by young adults and collectors of all age groups.

Loyal collectors are a valuable, focused target group so PEZ will be running a large collector's promotion this year. It also aims to encourage young children to build up their PEZ collection and become loyal collectors.

Other marketing channels include regular on-pack, print and online competitions to keep consumers involved with PEZ. Sampling promotions and cross promotions with other character licensees increase brand awareness. In addition, in 2005 PEZ dispensers were voted the 98th best gadget ever by the magazine Mobile PC.

What does the brand promise you?

The brand's success is based on its emphasis of high quality in terms of design and functionality. PEZ's constant new, top licensing themes from the world of cartoons and comic heroes make sure the characters retain their appeal to consumers.

Before licensing a character, PEZ carefully checks if the film story or comic behind the licence is appropriate for children. It's important for the brand's values that the story and character are not violent. PEZ's mission is to provide a unique toy, sweet and collectable in one to inspire children's imaginations and encourage sociable playing.

How was the brand developed?

Nearly 80 years ago, in Austria, Eduard Haas III developed a peppermint candy made of pressed sugar and peppermint oil that was marketed as the 'High Society Mint'. The German word for peppermint is PfeffErminZ, which is where the brand name 'PEZ' is derived from. During its first 10 years, the PEZ candy was geared exclusively towards adults.

The shape of the original PEZ candy has stayed the same since its launch in 1927, but now has a far reaching appeal. In addition, PEZ is available today in more flavours, including strawberry, lemon, orange and cherry in the UK.

The first PEZ dispenser was introduced in 1940, but again, it was targeted purely at adults with a product in the shape of a cigarette lighter. In 1952, small heads were put onto the dispensers. Ten years later, in 1962, Disney characters like Mickey Mouse, Donald Duck and Goofy made their first appearance on the top of the PEZ dispenser, giving the brand strong appeal to children. With each new series, the PEZ brand increasingly becomes a collector's item.

Did you know?

4.2 billion pieces of PEZ are consumed every year. Placed end to end, this quantity of sweets would be enough to circle the equator one and a half times.

The most expensive PEZ dispenser is 'Spare Froh', a mascot of an Austrian bank, from 1970. It recently sold for approximately US$1,500.

More than 65 million dispensers are sold annually around the globe and more than 4.2 billion single PEZ sweets are consumed each year.

PEZ made an appearance in the 1982 children's classic E.T., one of the biggest grossing films of all times.

PHILIPS

Philips' brand promise – sense and simplicity – ensures the mission to improve the quality of people's lives through the timely introduction of meaningful technological innovations is guided by the principles of sense and simplicity. Its message is simple and it is the backbone of the business. Philips aims to give its customers what they want through products that are simple to use which enhance their quality of life.

What is Philips Mother & Child Care?

Philips excels at producing pioneering and original products in three interlocking domains: healthcare, lifestyle and technology. In a world where technology increasingly touches every aspect of our daily lives, Philips is a world leader in both healthcare and consumer electronics. The scope of its healthcare business extends not only throughout the hospital, but beyond into the home and into all aspects of living a healthy life. Parents with young babies choose safety, reliability and user-friendliness as the most important decision factors in choosing baby care products. They expect that product developers meet their requirements with products that guarantee quality, safety and comfort.

Technology drives improvements in the healthcare business and Philips has a strong history of technological innovation. Over the last 110 years, Philips has created numerous innovations that have changed consumers lives, including the light bulb, the X-ray tube, audio communication, CDs, DVDs, HDTV, wearable electronics and near field communication.

Mother & Child Care is part of the global electronics company Philips and aims to tap into the growing trend of consumer health and well-being. Philips will be launching a new global product portfolio, which focuses on mother and child care, in the next few years. At the centre of all Philips design innovation is consumer insights, which are used to shape the development of all new products. The global electronics company always ensures that consumers are a priority when launching new innovative products.

The Mother & Child Care product portfolio centres around three main categories – food and nutrition, health and personal care and development and monitoring. The food and nutrition products aim to support mothers when feeding their babies and toddlers with products like food processors, unique steam nutrition centres (a combination of a steam steriliser, an ultra fast bottle warmer and a food steamer), sterilisers and fast bottle warmers.

The health and personal care products will help mothers diagnose and prevent common health concerns with products like thermometers and humidifiers.

Philips' development and monitoring product range focuses on helping parents monitor and measure what's happening with their child. These products include baby monitors, baby cams and location tracking devices.

Where would you have seen the brand?

Philips' existing products in the mother and child care market have already won a number of awards. Its DECT (Digital Enhanced Cordless Technology) baby monitor is a market leader in Western Europe and won a number of awards including the Mother & Baby Award in 2004 for the best monitor in the UK.

The awareness of Philips' DECT baby monitors has been boosted with an advertorial running in the Royal College of Midwives magazine, called 'Together we Care', with another one running this year. This is supported by banner advertising on its website.

Philips' magic mirror, which records and replays parents' and babies' own voices, won the Baby Product of the Year Award in the Netherlands in 2003. While the following year, Philips' wireless Babycam won the international CES Innovation Award. More recently, the new version of the DECT Baby Monitor launched in 2005 won the iF Product Design Award in the household and residential category.

Philips also promotes its brand through the sponsorship of the baby charity Tommy's events. Tommy's high profile with mothers, babies and the medical and healthcare professions boosts the awareness of Philips' Mother and Child Care range.

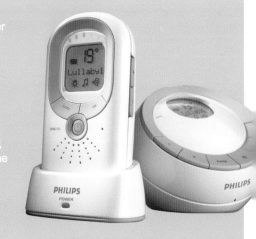

What does the brand promise you?

Philips Mother & Child Care pledges to help parents take care of the health and well-being of babies and children. This new division of the brand is building on Philips' heritage as an innovative, electronics specialist.

How was the brand developed?

In 1998, Philips Baby Care, the old name for the brand's Mother & Child Care division, introduced its first wireless baby monitor into Western Europe. Building on Philips' heritage of good quality control and design, the new product was targeted at babies from newborn to 18 months. The following year, Philips introduced its first nightlight, in co-operation with Miffy, a popular kids' character.

In 2000, Philips launched the Baby Care Institute to ensure it was generating the right innovations by speaking to first-time parents, nurseries, midwives, parenting magazines and specialist shops. Philips realised that there were no other specialists in electric baby appliances. The brand also decided to focus on parents who were likely to have recently had their first child and who both worked.

In the same year, Philips introduced a steam steriliser to help parents have enough sterilised bottles at hand throughout the day. It could be switched on at night and set to switch off automatically.

In 2001, Philips launched its award-winning DECT baby monitor, which reassures parents that no one else, aside from them, can listen into their baby sleeping. That year, it also expanded its portfolio into health and hygiene products with the launch of a thermometer set that could be sterilised before use.

Building on its innovative reputation, Philips has launched a number of firsts into the baby care market. They include a combined digital bath and room thermometer and the magic mirror, which stimulates a baby's development by recording and replaying parents' and babies' voices. In 2003, it launched a wireless, colour Babycam to reassure parents when they can't hear their baby.

In the last few years, Philips has consolidated its market leading role in DECT baby monitors with a new product range that also monitors the temperature in the baby's room and plays lullabies.

Did you know?

Philips is a global brand and keen to understand cultural differences between markets. While Chinese parents place emphasis on issues such as health, hygiene and safety, in the US, parents' focus is placed on speed and convenience.

Pizza Hut is one of the leading pizza restaurants and home delivery services in the UK. Offering freshly prepared food and value for money, Pizza Hut provides an informal family dining experience.

What is Pizza Hut?

Pizza Hut is the market leader in combined dine-in and off-premise sales in Britain's £2.5 billion pizza market. The brand has over 675 outlets nationally, including more than 415 dine-in restaurants and around 260 home-delivery units.

Offering good value for money, Pizza Hut is most famous for its popular lunchtime pizza buffet and unlimited ice cream factory as well as soft drink refills.

Where would you have seen the brand?

Pizza Hut restaurants and delivery outlets are located on high streets throughout the UK as well as out-of-town shopping centres. Consumers can also see the Pizza Hut brand in magazines, on TV and leaflets thanks to an aggressive PR, direct marketing and TV advertising campaign for all new product launches. Pizza Hut has also successfully linked up with children's animated films such as Chicken Run, The Grinch and Shrek.

In 2005, Pizza Hut was the winner of the baby charity Tommy's Parent Friendly Award for Best Family Restaurant. Across

the UK, over half a million parents voted for the awards, which recognise companies who help make parents' lives easier and less stressful.

Pizza Hut has a relaxed and informal attitude to dining with children and its restaurant facilities are designed with families in mind. For example, highchairs and baby-changing facilities are available. It also offers a good-value kids menu. Additionally, all young Pizza Hut customers receive special goody bags, which include an activity book and crayons. The introduction of a UK wide no-smoking policy at all restaurants in 2003 added to the restaurant's appeal for parents.

How was the brand developed?

The brand's story began in 1958 with two young brothers – Dan and Frank Carney. A family friend with the idea of opening a pizza parlour approached the brothers who borrowed £345 from their mother. They purchased second-hand equipment and rented a small building on a busy intersection in Wichita, Kansas, to launch the first Pizza Hut restaurant.

In the early days, when they were setting up, they only had room for 25 seats – and the restaurant sign only had space for nine letters. The Carney brothers knew they wanted 'Pizza' in the name, which left space for just three more letters. Because the building looked like a hut, the brand Pizza Hut was born.

By 1972, there were 1,000 Pizza Hut restaurants across the US. The following

year the brand launched internationally opening Pizza Huts in Canada, Japan and the UK. The first Pizza Hut UK opened in Islington, London and the brand grew quickly. By 1984, there were 50 Pizza Huts in the UK, two years later there were 100; in 1987 a new store was opening, on average, every week.

Pizza Hut UK now has 675 outlets in the UK and Ireland. It is undertaking an ongoing expansion process with 28 new stores opened in 2005. On a global scale, Pizza Hut is the largest pizza restaurant company in the world. It has 12,000 outlets in 90 countries, employing more than 300,000 people.

What does the
brand promise you?

Good value is at the heart of Pizza Hut's brand. It aims to offer a quality, casual dining experience close to 'fast food restaurant' prices.

The Pizza Hut brand reflects an upbeat, fun feel and the portions and atmosphere all reflect a love of Pizza.

Pizza Hut is renowned for its product innovation. In the UK the brand spends over £1 million every year on research and development. It responds to consumer demand by regularly updating its menu and offering new product innovations. In the last 10 years alone, Pizza Hut has built up an impressive record of product development and innovation, with the introduction of new concepts. In 1995, it introduced Stuffed Crust, which responded to the fact that children had traditionally left their pizza crusts in favour of the centre, by making the crusts more appealing with a cheese centre.

In 1997, the brand introduced The Sicilian, a flavoured base, and two years later it launched The Italian – a thin and light pizza which is hand-finished with flour. In April 2000, The Edge was born – the pizza without a crust, topped to the rim – followed

a year later by Twisted Crust. The Quad was then introduced in May 2002, with four different topping quarters making it ideal for sharing.

Two years later a new pizza called 4forALL was launched which offers four individual square pizzas in one – Margherita, Chicken Supreme, Pepperoni and Vegetable Supreme. Recently the Hi-Light healthier pizza has been introduced. It has a third less fat in its base compared to other Pizza Hut options.

There are ever-changing deals on the menu; the latest initiative has extended the buffet to seven days a week. Already popular with workers and students during the week, families and larger groups can now benefit at the weekend. March 2005 also saw the launch of a value deal offering every customer who buys a pizza, pasta, salad, starter or dessert, another of the same type at half price.

Did you
know?

An estimated 23% of the UK population have eaten a Pizza Hut pizza in the last 12 weeks.

In the last 30 years, Pizza Hut (UK) has sold 700 million pizzas.

Worldwide, Pizza Hut serves more than 1.7 million pizzas every day, to approximately four million customers.

Pizza Hut uses the equivalent of 525 million pounds of tomatoes each year and more than 700 million pounds of pepperoni per year to make its pizzas.

Celebrity fans of Pizza Hut include David and Victoria Beckham – Victoria Beckham recently went to Enfield Pizza Hut (January 2006) with her sons.

Breast, bottle or a combination of both? Controlled crying or continual comforting? What's safe (and what's not safe) to eat during pregnancy? How will a baby affect your relationship? Is my toddler's behaviour normal? How will my child cope on his first day at nursery?

Any first-time mum or mum-to-be will tell you there are hundreds of perplexing questions swimming around their heads during their first few years as a parent. With this in mind, Practical Parenting has been at hand to help, delivering reassurance and trusted advice since 1987.

What is Practical Parenting?

Practical Parenting is a monthly, glossy magazine designed specifically to support and inform parents and parents-to-be on their life-changing journey from pregnancy through to their child's first year at pre-school. Practical Parenting's friendly but expert advice covers all aspects of early parenting – including health, nutrition, development, play, sleeping and feeding – helping each reader make the best decisions for their young family.

Practical Parenting is one of the UK's leading parenting magazines. The monthly title was launched in 1987 and is a trusted brand with expertise in the parenting market. Its core readers are pregnant women or new mums with kids aged 0-5.

Practical Parenting prides itself on successfully marrying authoritative expert information with a warm, friendly and realistic approach to parenting.

The primary aim of the brand's editorial team is to identify and solve day-to-day problems and challenges faced by its readers, as well as to acknowledge and support them through any related emotional issues they may face.

Practical Parenting does this by offering practical and effective advice from experts and by sharing the wisdom of real life experience and hindsight from other parents who've been in similar situations. Product review and testing is also an important component of the magazine.

The BabyShows
in association with **parenting** magazine

www.thebabyshow.co.uk

Where would you have seen the brand?

Practical Parenting magazine is available on the newsstand and has also been the major media partner of The Baby Show, since the inaugural event launched in London in 2002.

The Baby Show, in association with Practical Parenting, is held in three different locations throughout each calendar year – Glasgow, Birmingham and London. It provides a unique opportunity for the brand's team to bring the magazine to life.

At each Baby Show, Practical Parenting readers and other visitors have the chance to meet the Practical Parenting experts as well as shop for all the leading pregnancy, baby and toddler products and services under one roof.

The magazine also publishes a series of books on a wide range of early parenting topics, in conjunction with book publisher Hamlyn. Topics of books previously published under the Practical Parenting brand include Sleeping, Settling, Tantrums and Development.

At the beginning of 2006, Practical Parenting's most recent book launches included Baby & Child: All Your Questions

Answered and Your Pregnancy Week By Week.

Practical Parenting's brand can also be viewed on TV. The magazine sponsors the twice-daily Pregnancy & Birth show on the Baby Channel. In addition, Practical Parenting editor Mara Lee took part in a Baby Channel feature called Yummy Mummy. She joined three other celebrity mums to discuss topical parenting issues as part of The Baby Channel's flagship magazine programme, Baby Talk.

The Practical Parenting brand also extends beyond the UK market, with successful monthly editions published in Australia. It is one of the leading parenting magazines in the Australian market.

How was the brand developed?

When Practical Parenting was launched in 1986, it was a spin-off of its sister title Family Circle, which is read by women with families. It was quickly realised that the magazine had potential on its own and the title was launched as a stand-alone monthly magazine soon after.

Nearly 20 years after the brand's launch, the magazine held its first annual awards in October 2005, the second awards are taking place this year sponsored by Fairy Bio. The Practical Parenting Awards are designed to celebrate parents, parenting professionals, and parenting products.

What does the brand promise you?

Practical Parenting offers its readers advice and guidance during the first few years of being a parent, a time when there are lots of questions and queries. This promise is reflected in the magazine's strap line: 'From pregnancy to pre-school, Practical Parenting is with you all the way!'

Practical Parenting delivers informative and accessible information on pregnancy, birth, babies, toddlers and pre-schoolers in a contemporary magazine format and tone. The title contains practical advice as well as real, honest and touching accounts of pregnancy and early parenting.

Practical Parenting is aimed at those who believe in the philosophy that being a mum doesn't stop them from being a woman. It's often a logical step forward for women who used to buy the monthly glossies before their pregnancy.

Above all else, the magazine aims to leave readers feeling privileged to be a parent, empowered to tackle any problems they have and part of a community that understands their day-to-day challenges.

Did you know?

Practical Parenting's most unusual cover line to date is: 'All I want for Christmas is a caesarean'.

The two topics most likely to prompt readers to write in and debate are caesarean versus natural delivery; and breastfeeding versus bottle feeding.

The most common request to the editorial team from readers is: Could my baby be on the front cover?

Famous contributors to Practical Parenting (past and present) include: Dr Miriam Stoppard; Supernanny Jo Frost; and baby food specialist, Annabel Karmel.

The most common reader photograph submitted to the magazine is a toddler on a potty reading Practical Parenting.

Pregnancy & birth

Pregnancy & birth magazine is the first destination for women seeking information and reassurance about their pregnancy. It is a fresh, up-to-date source of knowledge packed with useful content. The brand is the voice of pregnant women in the UK today and campaigns on a variety of issues including better antenatal care for British women.

What is Pregnancy & birth?

Pregnancy & birth is the best-selling pregnancy magazine in the UK. The sophisticated, monthly magazine is packed with information about pregnancy, health and well-being. It is practical, confidence-boosting and reassuring for mums-to-be. The brand is positioned as a friend for young expectant mums who want to know more about a wide range of issues – from the latest maternity fashion and the best pregnancy and baby buys, to dealing with embarrassing symptoms and relationship issues.

Pregnancy & birth prides itself on its broad appeal and in providing its pregnant readers with everything they need for a healthy, happy pregnancy, as well as relaying real-life experiences. Aside from pregnancy health coverage, its content includes the latest, prettiest, high street maternity fashions, plus a recently enlarged baby buys section to ensure readers are well informed when they buy the products they need for their new arrival.

Where would you have seen the brand?

Pregnancy & birth magazine is sold on newsstands nationwide, from supermarkets to small independent newsagents across the UK. Additionally, the brand is syndicated to four countries, while the UK magazine is sold in 30 countries worldwide.

Awareness of the brand is also boosted through features on its sister magazine's website www.motherandbabymagazine.com and cross-promotional advertising within other titles owned by Emap, its parent company.

Pregnancy & birth magazine has also achieved national media coverage as a result of its PR activity. This includes press interest in its 2005 Fertility Survey, which questioned 2,000 women in the UK, with an average age of 29. The results uncovered some shocking statistics about the attitudes and behaviour of couples trying to conceive and predicted a further decline in fertility for the future.

How was the brand developed?

Pregnancy & birth began life as a special supplement in Mother & Baby, its sister magazine. It was so well received that the

brand was launched as a separate monthly magazine in 1984. Since then, it has gone from strength to strength and is now the biggest-selling pregnancy magazine in the UK (ABC J-D05). Guided by its new editor, Sarah Hart, the magazine has just been redesigned to make it fresher, more

modern and exciting, to appeal to today's expectant mums.

The brand has also been extended into other products. In 2003, it launched the Pregnancy & birth Wellbeing CD for distribution across retail outlets. The triple CD features music to inspire and relax listeners during pregnancy, as well as a sleep CD to help soothe newborns into a peaceful nights sleep.

This year, the Pregnancy & birth brand is extending further with the launch of its first annual awards. The fashion & beauty awards aim to recognise and honour some of the best maternity fashion brands and beauty products in the market. Pregnancy & birth have also introduced the Editors Choice stamp which promotes products that the magazine feel are the best for its readers.

What does the brand promise you?

Pregnancy & birth is a real, inclusive, celebratory brand that appeals to new mothers at an exciting time in their lives. The brand also aims to act as a confidence-building tool for its readers. This is because of the practical, informative, trustworthy advice it offers.

According to its strap line, Pregnancy & birth is a brand that can become your best friend in pregnancy. This is because it celebrates with its readers as well as delivering advice, reassurance, empathy and support to them.

Did you know?

Pregnancy & birth was born within a Mother & Baby magazine special issue.

Pregnancy & birth is often the first thing a newly pregnant woman buys, that is, after a pregnancy test.

185,000 pregnant women read Pregnancy & birth every month.

Pregnancy & birth has a picture library of over 3,000 quality specialist images, which it sells worldwide.

Sainsbury's Kids is a new healthier food range for kids with an emphasis on nutritional balance. It offers healthier food products that appeal to children and that parents will trust.

What is Sainsbury's Kids?

Sainsbury's Kids is a healthier range of food with over 80 products. It replaces the supermarket's current kids' range, Blue Parrot Café. The range is targeted towards children aged 5-10 years-old.

The range sees Sainsbury's become the first supermarket to remove cartoon characters from its own-label children's food. Instead, the emphasis is placed on nutritional information and images of real children enjoying their food.

Sainsbury's is the first retailer to publish recommended guidelines for children on the packaging, to help parents make informed choices about their kids' nutrition. Traditionally, Guidance Daily Amounts (GDAs) for adults have been printed on the back of packaging, but have not included advice about children. However, children's nutritional needs are often very different. For example, kids need the same amount of saturated fat every day as an average woman but much lower levels of salt. Sainsbury's packaging including details of children's GDAs will begin with the kids range and eventually extend to all own brand products.

Parents can prepare healthier lunchboxes with mini bagels and wholemeal rolls which are ideal for little mouths and include extra fibre. They can also include dairy pouches and tubes – a fun way for parents to introduce more calcium into kids' diets. The range also offers squeezy tubes of whole milk yoghurt, with a natural source of Omega-3 that may enhance learning and concentration and mini cucumber served with humous.

Meanwhile Sainsbury's Kids Water and Sainsbury's Kids Juicy Water offer a healthier alternative for packed lunches.

Sainsbury's Kids Water uses a sport cap to restrict spillages and Juicy Water, available in apple or banana, has a 75% juice content. A healthier alternative to a bag of crisps comes in the form of humous and breadstick dippers. Similarly, a carrot, celery, cucumber and fromage frais lunchbox dip contains one portion of vegetables.

In the evening, Sainsbury's Kids aims to help parents make nutritious meals for their children easily. The range includes Pizza Fingers, Fish Nuggets, Kids Easy Steam Vegetables, as well as ready meals for busy families with no additives or preservatives. Its beef and vegetable burgers contain mashed vegetables to help kids eat their recommended five portions of fruit or vegetable a day.

Where would you have seen the brand?

The brand was launched at the end of February 2006. The new children's range is available at selected Sainsbury's supermarkets across the UK. The brand is being promoted in-store, with special attention focused on the ready meals, yoghurt, drinks and frozen food aisles. It is also being marketed with an introductory 20% off promotion. The brand's awareness is also being boosted with sampling campaigns.

The brand's launch also tied into a new scheme by Sainsbury's to donate sports equipment to schools, a promotion called Active Kids. The Sainsbury's Kids range forms part of the bonus vouchers scheme, which includes any product which has a stamp in the shape of an apple.

The range ties into Sainsbury's commitment to family health. This has been supported by a high profile marketing campaign which focused on family health and ran across all channels including TV, press, direct marketing and PR.

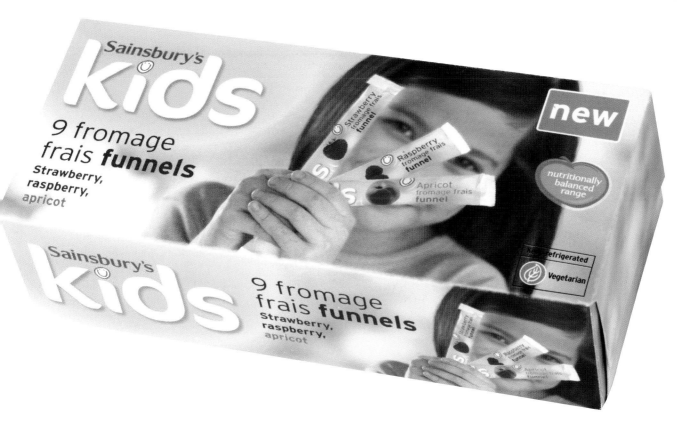

How was the brand developed?

Research showed that parents were becoming increasingly concerned about the foods their children were eating both in and out of school. The media focus on children's health was increasing with headlines suggesting approximately 4% of young people were obese, while a further 15% were classified as overweight.

Sainsbury's was aware that parents' time constraints meant that they often look for easier solutions, particularly on week nights, rather than preparing fresh meals for their kids. In addition, consumers were becoming increasingly choosy about the food and drink they bought for their kids but were also confused about the proliferation of health messages.

Building on the Blue Parrot Café brand that Sainsbury's launched in 2001, the Sainsbury's Kids range placed emphasis on healthy eating to make it simpler for parents keen to feed their children nutritious food.

What does the brand promise you?

Sainsbury's Kids pledges to make life easier for young families by offering healthier meals and snacks for kids. The entire range has been developed with good nutrition in mind. This means that there are no hydrogenated fats in the products and that other fats, sugar and salt are strictly controlled.

The range, which was taste tested by children, also contains no artificial colours and flavours, and only contains colours approved by the Hyperactive Children's Support Group. Sainsbury's Kids aims to ensure that it does not cost young families more to eat healthily.

Did you know?

Recent TNS data shows that following the TV programme, Jamie's School Dinners, nearly 60% of women with children actively look out for healthy products when shopping.

Only 10%, of those questioned, say they are not worried about providing their children with healthy foods (Source: TNS).

Fifteen different children were used on the packaging of the 80 products in the range.

Products in the range were taste tested on a group of school children in the Wirral, Cheshire.

Silver Cross is the oldest and only British pram manufacturer in the UK today. For the last 130 years, the brand has been providing prams, pushchairs and travel systems for young families.

Based in Skipton, Yorkshire, the brand is passionate about offering parents the highest levels of baby comfort and safety with stylish and innovative design at the best possible value. Built to traditional standards with every raw material and process checked by in-house engineers, Silver Cross provides the level of quality you would expect from a trusted British brand.

What is Silver Cross?

Silver Cross offers a comprehensive collection of top quality travel systems suitable for a newborn baby through to toddler. The range is split into the Lifestyle and Heritage collection.

The new Lifestyle collection was launched in 2003. It currently includes three award-winning travel systems designed to suit today's lifestyle. This includes the Classic Sleepover, a unique pram, pushchair and carrycot in one; the Linear Freeway, which is the sleekest and lightest combination pushchair Silver Cross has ever made; and the Cruiser, which has maximum versatility, design and comfort – ideal for a newborn.

The Lifestyle collection also includes two car seats, the Ventura Infant Carrier, an award-winning, comfortable, technologically advanced car seat for a newborn; and the Explorer, a two-stage car seat that grows with your child and uses a seat belt tensioning system.

Silver Cross' Heritage collection builds on the brand's 130 year history. It includes two traditional coach-style prams and a range of collectable toys for young children. The iconic coach prams are still handmade today to the same exacting standards as they were in the 19th century.

The Balmoral is a pram highly favoured by the royals and desired by celebrities for its looks and freely suspended body providing a very comfortable ride for babies. Each iconic pram has an individually numbered plaque and certificate of authenticity including the craftsman's signature. The Kensington is a classic pram and is defined by a hand painted steel body and highly-polished chrome chassis.

Silver Cross' range of collectable toys includes the Oberon, a handmade doll's pram. In 2006, two limited edition Oberons featuring Peter Rabbit and Winnie the Pooh, were also produced. The Merlin, a rocking horse hand carved from solid ash, and created by an artist, has real horse hair and leather straps and saddle. Only 100 have ever been made.

Where would you have seen the brand?

Silver Cross has been a familiar and well-loved brand for generations. It has also been a British royal favourite since 1870 and used by a succession of royal babies. With a heavily invested and highly targeted advertising and PR campaign the brand is going from strength to strength.

The popularity of the lifestyle range is growing annually, partly due to its reputation amongst the parenting media world, mothers and its celebrity status. Silver Cross has a new following of celebrities who endorse the brand including Penny Lancaster, Britney Spears, Gwyneth Paltrow, Sarah Jessica Parker, Kate Hudson, Madonna and Kate Moss.

The growing recognition of the British brand across the globe, aided by celebrity endorsement has been pivotal in launching Silver Cross in four key global markets. From the beginning of 2006, the brand will be marketed in the US, Canada, Australia and Japan.

Silver Cross is aiming for an increased share in sales of all wheeled goods worldwide in the next five years – a business that is currently worth in excess of US$1 billion. The focus for Silver Cross this year will be to offer new parents, across the globe, an international selection of quality nursery products.

Last year, the lifestyle range was put through its paces by parents across the UK. It won 20 high profile parenting magazine awards in just one year, plus a Silver for Best Pushchair in the Mother & Baby 2005 annual awards and Editors Choice in the Prima Baby Reader Awards.

How was the brand developed?

Silver Cross was founded in 1877 by William Wilson, a prolific inventor of baby carriages. By the time of his death in 1913, William had been granted over 30 patents.

In 1898 a purpose built factory was opened in Silver Cross Street in Leeds and was named the 'Silver Cross Works'. In the 1920s and 1930s Silver Cross became incorporated and crowned the number one baby carriage for royals, supplying its first baby carriage to the Princess Royal.

During World War II the main part of the Silver Cross factory was requisitioned by the Air Ministry, producing over 16 million aircraft parts for the war effort. The experience gained during the war years was applied to production methods and the traditional plywood body was replaced with aluminium.

Over the years the pram shapes have altered with social conditions and fashions dictating styling and colours. Harrods was home for the 2002 re-launch of the famous Balmoral with stars such as Catherine Zeta Jones, Sarah Jessica Parker, Elizabeth Hurley and Brooke Shields becoming proud owners.

A year later the new Lifestyle Collection arrived. Two new additions to this collection will include: the 3D – a fully lie flat pram, stroller and travel system in one; and the S4 – a smart, urban three-wheeler soon to hit the streets.

Did you know?

Silver Cross is the oldest British nursery brand having been founded in 1877.

More than 1,000 single hand operations are required to make a Balmoral pram.

During World War II the Silver Cross factory was requisitioned by the air ministry to manufacture aircraft machine parts – this experience revolutionised pram design.

Silver Cross prams are sold in over 20 countries worldwide.

Silver Cross prams are the most featured traditional prams in Hollywood films.

75,000 Silver Cross prams are sold globally each year.

What does the brand promise you?

All Silver Cross travel systems aim to address the changing needs of modern parents, while meeting the highest standards of safety and comfort. Silver Cross continues its history of exceeding expectations with high quality, fashionable and innovative nursery products at affordable prices.

Today almost one in two mums in the UK and the Republic of Ireland use SMA Nutrition products and it continues to be the leader in infant nutrition (Source: IRI, ACNielsen and TNS – MAT October 2005). The company has been looking after infant and toddler nutrition for over 80 years and has a wealth of experience on hand to help mothers.

What is SMA Nutrition?

From the beginning, feeding a baby is inextricably linked with trust, love and caring as well as providing nourishment to help a child grow and develop properly. Breast feeding with all its natural advantages is held up as the gold standard. In recognising this, SMA Nutrition has built a brand with as similar functional benefits as possible to breast milk, to help bottle feeding parents take care of their baby. SMA* is the most popular baby milk brand in the UK and Republic of Ireland (Source: IRI, ACNielsen and TNS – MAT October 2005).

Where would you have seen the brand?

The SMA Nutrition products are widely distributed in hospitals, pharmacies, supermarkets and grocery outlets. Promotional activity direct to consumers is restricted to SMA Progress*, which is suitable for babies from six months to two years-old. SMA Progress is advertised on TV and radio, and in the parenting press.

Through extensive research SMA Nutrition has gained valuable insight into consumer needs and understands the emotional and practical realities of parenthood. As a consequence the SMA Careline*, a telephone support service for parents and healthcare professionals, was launched in 1997. It offers knowledgeable, unbiased information on an increasing range of parent and baby issues together with the latest guidelines recommended by experts in the baby milk market. A comprehensive variety of literature and booklets ranging from information on pregnancy through to infant nutrition and potty training is also available.

The SMA Careline understands that every baby is different and real life does not always match the text books, as a result sound practical information can be sought. It's staffed by a friendly team (with back-up from qualified healthcare professionals) who have experience in parenthood and midwifery as well as a genuinely caring attitude.

In addition to SMA Nutrition's innovative product development is a range of quality services and support including the SMA Mums' Network*. This consists of an interactive, personalised website and a range of helpful hints and tips from pregnancy to toddlerhood in the form of a planner and information booklets.

At SMA Nutrition's website (www.smanutrition.co.uk) and via the SMA Mums' Network, consumers can find free, valuable and practical information to guide them along the important milestones of motherhood. From their first month with the bump to enjoying the little-one's first steps, SMA Mums' Network provides a number of free services. It enables pregnant mums to keep track of their current situation based on their due date and set up their own online, personalised profile to help them prepare for what's ahead with practical guidance from real mothers.

How was the brand developed?

In 1911, the American paediatrician, Dr Henry J. Gerstenberger had a vision to create an infant milk formula with a composition nutritionally and biologically similar to that of human milk. With this ambition in mind, he developed a product called SMA, derived from the phrase Synthetic Milk Adapted. Several years later the first commercial product was launched.

What does the brand promise you?

When mothers choose SMA Nutrition they are reassured that their bottle-fed baby is being given a good start in life. Also, because SMA Nutrition has a deep understanding of mums-to-be and parents' needs, mothers are able to benefit from the invaluable support of its dedicated, experienced professionals from pre-conception, until their child becomes a toddler.

Since then SMA Nutrition has remained firmly at the forefront of meeting the nutritional needs of babies and toddlers. This requires a team of nutritional experts working continuously to pioneer new scientific developments to improve baby milk, and introduce innovative, new products.

This level of commitment and expertise has enabled SMA Nutrition to achieve a number of significant firsts in UK baby milk history. These include being the first company to introduce a ready-to-feed system for use in maternity units and at home, the first whey-dominant formula and the first follow-on milk. SMA Nutrition has also innovated in the baby milk sector in terms of packaging. It was the first brand available in tins, the first to launch ready-to-use milk in small bottles for hospitals and cartons for home use, as well as a convenient sachet format for individual feeds.

As far as the future is concerned, SMA Nutrition is currently working on a range of new products and reformulations. It is also continually re-evaluating and updating its parent and healthcare professional support programme to suit changing trends in baby and toddler care.

Did you know?

More first-time mothers in the UK choose SMA Nutrition than any other baby milk (Source: TNS – six months ending December 4th 2005).

SMA Nutrition was the first brand, in 1961, to develop a whey protein formula balanced in the same ratio as breast milk.

Since its introduction in 1997, the SMA Careline has helped over 200,000 parents and healthcare professionals.

SMA Nutrition was the first company to introduce a convenient, ready-to-feed liquid.

*Trade mark
ZCO 0272/02/06

IMPORTANT NOTICE: Breast feeding is best for babies. Good maternal nutrition is important for the preparation and maintenance of breast feeding. Introducing partial bottle feeding may have a negative effect on breast feeding and reversing a decision not to breast feed is difficult. Professional advice should be followed on infant feeding. Social and financial implications should be considered when selecting a method of infant feeding. SMA PROGRESS is a follow-on milk for babies over six months and is not intended to replace breast feeding. When used in conjunction with solid feeding, it provides the nourishment essential to a baby's healthy and sustained growth.

Speedo is synonymous with the experience of swimming, from childhood lessons and holidays to the Olympic Games. Founded in Australia in 1928, Speedo is the world's leading swimwear brand in more than 170 countries worldwide.

What is Speedo?

As the market leader in kids' swimwear, Speedo is constantly seeking new ways to encourage children to learn and enjoy swimming. Not only is it a fun way to exercise, it's also an important life-saving skill.

Speedo understands the importance and process of learning to swim from a young age. Through working with the best swimmers and coaches, Speedo has identified three key stages to maximise a child's potential in water and designed products for each stage:

Stage one is when the child first experiences water and it's important that they feel comfortable and at ease in the swimming pool. The Speedo Baby Seat provides the correct amount of buoyancy and security to help a child grow in confidence at this early stage.

Stage two is the introduction to swimming. Speedo products have been designed to help with the process of learning to swim, and assist buoyancy while encouraging the child to adopt the correct swimming position. This range includes the Speedo Bobble Armband, which doesn't need inflating.

Stage three focuses on developing the child's water confidence and their ability to swim using fun activities such as Dive Shapes and the Hungry Shark Game. These games encourage the child to dive and grow in confidence using their skills.

There is a growing awareness that overexposure to sunlight can lead to potentially damaging effects such as sunburn, premature signs of ageing and an increased risk of skin cancer. This is why Speedo's Spring/Summer 2006 Tots collection for 1-6 year-olds has extended into Sun Protection clothing. The range has an ultraviolet protection factor of 50+, the highest possible rating of UV ray protection for clothing.

The composition and weave density of the fabric used in Speedo's Sun Protection range means it blocks UV radiation much more effectively than traditional clothing or swimwear. This is why it has been awarded the CE mark of excellence for meeting stringent European standards for solar UV-protective properties.

An understanding of consumer needs is at the heart of all Speedo products. For example, Speedo understands the importance of providing long-lasting swimwear for children who swim regularly.

The Speedo Endurance® collection is made of a high performance fabric that does not degrade in chlorinated water and lasts much longer than conventional nylon/Lycra® fabric. Available for tots up to teens, Endurance® suits also keep their shape, are quick drying and are 20 times more colour resistant.

Where would you have seen the brand?

Speedo products are sold in over 4,000 stores across the UK in retailers such as JJB, JD, Debenhams, Boots, adams kids and Toys R Us as well as leading independents. In 2005, the brand launched a new store design at its European flagship store in Covent Garden, London. The design will be rolled out to over 300 stores across the world in the next two years and has won the 2005 Retail Interior Award for Best Small Shop Design.

Sponsorship plays a central role in Speedo's marketing strategy. On a global scale, Speedo has a number of endorsees including American Michael Phelps, the first swimmer in history to win eight medals during one Olympic Games. He was a key figure launching the Fastskin FSII suit, which he wore in Athens and was featured in the supporting communications. On a national scale, Speedo is a proud sponsor of the British Swimming Association. It supports all water disciplines and levels of ability from grass roots to the elite team squad.

How was the brand developed?

In Australia, in the late 1920s, a more liberal attitude to mixed swimming and a growing interest in the sport provided the necessary backdrop for Speedo's birth. In 1928 a staff competition to name the new swimwear brand spawned the slogan, 'Speed on in your Speedo's' at the MacRaes Knitting Mills in Sydney.

In the 1930s and 1940s Speedo became the favoured brand for competitive swimmers. It was the first brand to introduce a revolutionary fabric containing nylon and elastane, which to this day remains the staple fabric of swimwear.

Following success at the Olympic Games, Speedo soon became a credible global phenomenon. The brand's Olympic presence has continued to grow and at the 2004 Athens Games, five out of eight World Records and 18 out of 26 Olympic Records were broken by swimmers wearing Speedo. More swimmers in Athens wore Speedo than all the other brands together.

Although Speedo's roots lie in competition swimwear, the brand has also introduced designer beach and leisure wear collections. In 2003, to celebrate the brand's 75th anniversary, swimwear designer Melissa Odabash created a range of swimsuits that were modelled by Naomi Campbell and Jodie Kidd and photographed by Bryan Adams.

Following the success of this collaboration, Speedo joined forces with Brazilian swimwear designer Rosa Cha to launch a range of designer beachwear as part of its Spring/Summer 2005 collection. In Spring/Summer 2006, Speedo will launch a unique collaboration with Comme des Garcon, which was initially unveiled at Paris Fashion Week.

Did you know?

More athletes swam in Speedo products at the 2004 Athens Olympics than all the other brands put together.

Over two million pairs of Speedo goggles are sold in the UK every year.

At the 2004 Athens Olympic Games, Speedo endorsee Michael Phelps won eight medals, the most medals won by any swimmer in one Olympic Games.

Speedo has patented the new Bobble armband, a unique foam armband that doesn't need inflating.

What does the brand promise you?

Speedo is a water expert. Its products are designed to help consumers look and feel their best, whether they are competing, training for health, having fun or just relaxing. The brand is renowned for innovation, best fit, quality, performance and, fundamentally, trust. With over 75 years of swimwear experience, Speedo plans to rule the pool for many years to come.

Sun-Pat peanut butter, has been a popular British brand since it was first produced in the UK in 1960. Sun-Pat is Britain's favourite peanut butter, with 300 million Sun-Pat sandwiches or rounds of toast eaten every year.

What is Sun-Pat?

The combination of Sun-Pat's range and recipe, in its distinctive packaging makes Sun-Pat one of the UK's most popular spreads. Sun-Pat's main ingredient, peanuts, provides a nutritious source of energy and is particularly high in protein, is a good source of fibre and folic acid and has a low GI index.

The brand can be found in five different variations. Sun-Pat Crunchy, which is the classic crunchy peanut butter. Sun-Pat Smooth, which is the classic – minus the crunch. Then, Sun-Pat Extra Crunchy and Sun-Pat Super Smooth and finally the most recent variety, which is called Sun-Pat Organic Crunchy.

Sun-Pat Peanut Butter is typically made from Virginia or Runner varieties of peanut, which give the best flavour to the spread. The nuts can come from a variety of sources such as North, Central or South America, or alternatively from Australia.

The peanuts are first roasted to the desired colour, which adds to the flavour of the final product, and then the skin is removed. A little sugar, salt and stabiliser (to keep the oil from separating) is added, and the ingredients are fed into a mill and ground to a smooth paste. For a crunchy texture, kibbled peanuts are added. Then the jars are filled, sealed and labelled, before making their way to a shop.

Where would you have seen the brand?

Sun-Pat has been widely advertised on TV, using campaigns with notable strap lines. These have included, 'What is the nuttiest thing you've ever done?' and 'He's a nutter'. One of the most memorable strap lines, 'Our son, Pat,' played on double-meanings to end with the phrase, 'sun-packed, fun-packed, our Sun-Pat'.

As children are among the peanut butter's most fervent fans, they often feature in the brand's marketing. One 1970s press ad confidently promised parents that: 'Your kids will love the real peanut taste of Sun-Pat.' A later ad in the 1990s featured a butcher in a striped apron, holding a meat cleaver and a string of sausages. He whispered the secret to readers that Sun-Pat contains more protein than chicken, turkey or beef.

How was the brand developed?

In the early 1890s, a doctor from Michigan in America developed peanut butter as a nutritious and easy-to-eat food. He was looking for a protein-rich food for people who could not chew meat because of the poor state of their teeth.

He decided to try feeding them crushed peanuts, because of their 25% protein content. Before long his peanut paste was selling well in local shops and by the mid 1890s the new product provoked the attention of the Kellogg brothers.

John Kellogg, a doctor and vegetarian, was credited with developing peanut butter. He took out a patent for the 'Process of Preparing Nut Meal' in 1895 that described the product as 'a pasty adhesive substance that is for convenience of distinction termed nut butter'. However, he steamed his peanuts rather than roasting them, and his spread did not taste like today's peanut butter.

While breakfast cereal made Kellogg a household name, other companies focused on peanut butter. By the 20th century, no kitchen cupboard in America was complete without a jar of peanut butter.

The peanut spread market remained confined to the US for many years. This was partly because the peanuts were grown in

Sun-Pat is a registered trade mark.

the southern American states of Georgia, Alabama and Florida, and also because peanut butter brands were only being sold in America.

The British had to wait for 40 years before they could taste peanut butter sandwiches – the staple diet of school children all across the States. Peanut butter was first sold in the UK in the 1930s. But, it wasn't until 1960 that the Sun-Pat company first started to produce Sun-Pat in Hadfield, as a by-product of a nut packing operation.

Since then the brand has evolved, launching new products for its consumers. In the 1990s Sun-Pat launched Sun-Pat American Style, which was later re-launched as Sun-Pat Creamy. These varieties no longer exist as Sun-Pat has refined its range to keep up to date with consumers demands and expectations. Another historical product variety that existed in the mid 1990s was Sun-Pat Chocanut which was a 'wicked' combination of peanut butter and chocolate spread.

What does the brand promise you?

The first part of Sun-Pat's brand name links it to the idea of providing energy. 'Sun' also suggests brightness, cheeriness, vibrancy and goodness, all values that are developed in the primary red and yellow colours and the sunburst motifs of the current label design. Meanwhile, although peanut butter is not a milk-based butter, the second part of the brand name 'Pat' hints at the traditional values of butter.

Sun-Pat peanut butter has been providing sound family nutrition and healthy goodness since 1960.

Sylvanian Families is a collection of woodland animal families for children to play with and collect. Sylvanian Families allows children to use their imagination within the comfort of a family environment.

Due to the collectible nature of the products, there are many adult collectors across the world. Unlike other faddish children's toys, Sylvanian Families is a long-lasting brand that is not dictated by fashion. The idea of family and the world of Sylvania can be as relevant today as it was 20 years ago when the brand launched.

What is Sylvanian Families?

Sylvanian Families' collection of woodland animals comes in family units of mother, father, brother, sister and babies. The characters dressed in different clothing each have their own name, character and story line. There is a wide variety of families within the brand's world including rabbits, badgers, bears, squirrels, foxes, hedgehogs, as well as reindeers, hound dogs, otters and owls.

Since the launch of the Sylvanian Families brand, nearly 20 years ago, there have been over 500 characters in the world of Sylvania. In 2005, the most popular characters were the Buttermilk Rabbit Family and the White Mouse Family. The New Dale Sheep Family, introduced in 2006, are also expected to become favourites.

Children can also house their families in cosy detached homes, Ivy Cottage and Riverside Lodge to grander houses like Willow Hall and Oakwood Manor House. The families can also be provided with a full range of accessories and detailed furniture, from the Cottage Kitchen Set to the Victorian Living Room Set, along with additional play sets including canal boats, caravans and buses.

Sylvanian Families offers a blend of traditional family life play. The brand incorporates memorable characters and incredible detail that young girls are known to like. Around six new families are introduced each year to ensure collectability. This means that current trends are taken into account but never at the expense of the brand's identity.

As the new licensing programme gets underway there will be even more Sylvanian Families products to add to the collection. Sylvanian Families is a very popular concept for young girls, especially from four to eight years old. This brand's appeal also extends up to early teens. Younger children like to play, while older children build up collections and create settings in their bedrooms.

Where would you have seen the brand?

Sylvanian Families has a multi-channel marketing strategy to promote the brand. It creates new TV advertising annually in order to build consumer awareness and promote new products. Last year's TV spot featured a key product in the 2005 range called Willow Hall – a house with lights, which ran from August until November. The next TV campaign will break in Easter, featuring the new Spring Time in Sylvania range and the new Dale Sheep Family.

The brand also runs press advertising in appropriate children's magazines. These press ads can include cover mounts, story strips and full or half-page competitions, as well as the sponsorship of letters pages.

Other marketing includes sampling, promotions, and advertising on children's websites, as well as sponsorships and consumer competitions. Sylvanian characters also appear in consumer catalogues and on collectors' posters.

Last year, the brand extended into experiences, with the first-ever Sylvanian Families Showtime Weekend Event at the Hop Farm Country Park in Kent. The woodland creatures appeared in a full stage show which was supported by sing-a-longs, games and competitions throughout the weekend.

The brand's fans could also enjoy Sylvanian characters face painting, Sylvanian story telling, a special Sylvanian Treasure Hunt and the opportunity to be photographed with the life size Sylvanian caravan and

Sylvanian Families brand values include family
values, nurturing, cosy, timeless, wholesome,
longevity and play-driven.

Did you know?

Sylvanian Families gets its
name from the word sylvan,
meaning 'of woods, woodland
and forest'.

**The earlier style Sylvanian
Families figures had flat hands
that could not hold anything.**

In 2007, Sylvanian Families
will be celebrating its 20th
anniversary.

**Since the launch of the
Sylvanian Families brand there
have been over 500 characters
in the world of Sylvania.**

The country cottage was the
first house to be launched
in 1987.

**Children can now visit life-size
Sylvanian houses, restaurants
and shops at the Sylvanian
Families Theme Park in Japan,
which was launched in 2004.**

pony. The Best Dressed Sylvanian Character
visitor to the show received a special prize
and the Sylvanian Collectors Club was
present to attract new membership.

Sylvanian Families also holds annual,
national competitions to persuade young
consumers to interact with the brand.
These have included Search for a Star and
Name the Bear Family competitions.

Retail stores also offer promotions and
competitions to market the brand. Some
shops hire life-sized costumes of the
favourite Sylvanian characters. The brand
is also boosted through in-store colouring
competitions, product displays and
leaflets. There is an annual window display
competition with the independent retail
chain Toymaster.

Sylvanian Families is also the only brand
to have ever won the BTHA Toy of the Year
award three years in a row in 1987, 1988
and 1989. It was also recently awarded the
2005 Toy Retailers Association Toy Range
of the Year award.

How was the brand developed?
Sylvanian Families was originally launched
in Japan in 1984. Three years later the
children's brand was launched in the UK.

Sylvanian Families Licensing arm has
recently been launched, which aims to build
on the success of the toy brand to create a
complementary range of products in key
categories. It is hoped this will create a
long-term, sustainable licensing programme
to enhance the brand and reflect its values.

The
Children's
Mutual™

Where money grows up

www.thechildrensmutual.co.uk

The Children's Mutual helps parents provide financial security for their children's future. It is widely regarded as an expert in long-term savings for kids and is the only UK company that specialises exclusively in saving for children.

What is The Children's Mutual?

The Children's Mutual is a financial services brand which offers a range of savings products to help meet the different requirements of parents and grandparents saving for children and grandchildren. Some of these products can enable them to take advantage of tax breaks, or to utilise savings for children as part of their inheritance tax planning.

The Children's Mutual's current core products are share-based stakeholder and non-stakeholder Child Trust Fund accounts. These accounts derive from a new Government initiative to help provide all eligible children born since September 2002 with a financial springboard into adult life. Intended, as announced by Chancellor Gordon Brown, to encourage savings for children, the Child Trust Fund (CTF) scheme was launched in January 2005, with the first accounts being opened in April 2005. The Children's Mutual played an important role in assisting the Government during its consultation process on the scheme.

Parents of over 2.5 million babies born since September 2002 have received a voucher for at least £250 from the Government, to be used to open a CTF account, into which additional savings can be made for their child.

In addition to its CTF accounts, The Children's Mutual has also launched the Growing Up Bond, a share-based investment plan which is specifically designed for parents or grandparents wishing to make additional savings for their children or grandchildren, outside of the CTF.

Additionally in 2005, The Children's Mutual launched a Shariah Baby Bond® stakeholder Child Trust Fund account following wide consultation with the Muslim Community. This financial product recognises that a significant number of Muslim parents want to be able to access the advantages of the CTF scheme in a way that complies with their faith.

Where would you have seen the brand?

Products in The Children's Mutual's range are either available direct from the company or via financial advisers. In order to help ensure potential customers are offered savings products that are suitable for their needs, the brand works closely with financial advisers to provide their clients with guidance about saving for children in the long term. Indeed, the brand won a Financial Adviser 5-Star Service Award for the ninth time running in 2004 and a 4-Star Award in 2005.

Additionally, as part of its marketing strategy, The Children's Mutual has developed strategic partnerships with other organisations to help open up access to its products – particularly its stakeholder Child Trust Fund account – to the customer in the high street. These partners include Boots, Mothercare, Lloyds TSB, CIS, AXA and a number of building societies tied to Norwich Union for investment products.

How was the brand developed?

The organisation behind The Children's Mutual brand has a long and distinguished history. Established in 1881, the Tunbridge Wells Equitable Friendly Society (TWEFS) was formed partly in response to the changing world of the Victorians when Government support for working people in hardship was negligible.

People created friendly societies to provide financial support to members who wished to contribute. Friendly societies delivered the first welfare provisions in the early part of the 20th century and were an important element in providing savings and protection for ordinary people. They continued to work with the state in administering significant parts of the National Health Service in its early years.

With the advent of financial services regulation in the 1980s, and immense competition during the 1990s, smaller independent financial service providers such as TWEFS found the market increasingly more difficult to operate in.

What does the brand promise you?

The Children's Mutual's aim is to help parents ensure their children are financially well equipped for the future. It seeks to achieve this by offering a range of flexible, long-term savings products that parents and grandparents can use to help provide a financial head-start for their children and grandchildren.

During the late 1990s TWEFS critically analysed the market and its product range, which included Baby Bond®, the well-known with-profits savings plan for children. This revealed that customers valued the society's role in providing a safe home for savings when planning for their children's future.

As a result of this analysis the organisation was radically reformed and The Children's Mutual brand was launched as its new trading name in January 2003. The brand launch was supported by thorough internal and external communications programmes. These included a cultural change programme for employees and extensive media activity.

The fundamental objective of the re-launch was to place expertise in long-term savings for children at the heart of the organisation.

The company already had in-depth experience of this segment of the market and it had in fact introduced its first children's savings plan in 1948.

The 2003 brand launch was well-timed. The increasing cost of university education, the overheated housing market and the general rising costs associated with young people starting adult life, have all heightened public and media awareness of the need to start making financial provision for a child's future at an early age.

In a short period of time The Children's Mutual has achieved its ambition to become considered as expert in its chosen field. Journalists, regulators, Government, customers and other key opinion formers increasingly view the brand as a leading specialist in helping families with children to become financially equipped for the future.

Did you know?

Prior to the launch of the Child Trust Fund scheme around one in five parents regularly put aside money for their children; this number has more than doubled.

Many people fear that if you save on behalf of a child and let them have the lump sum when they reach 18 they will spend the money inappropriately. However, The Children's Mutual research shows that the majority of young people actually spend the money on what it was intended for.

Tixylix

Tixylix® is the number one children's cough and cold medicine in the UK (Source: IRI HBA All Outlets 52 W/E December 24th 2005). With a heritage spanning over 45 years, generations of mums have turned to Tixylix to help quickly soothe the uncomfortable symptoms of coughs and colds for their kids.

What is Tixylix?

Tixylix is a cough and cold remedy range specially designed for children. This means it is the only cough and cold brand which purely focuses on providing first class soothing remedies suitable for children aged from three months to 10 years-old.

It can be difficult to persuade children to take medicine but Tixylix products are pleasant-tasting. Meanwhile parents can be reassured because they're also sugar-free.

Tixylix has a range of children's cough and cold medicines suitable for different age groups and a variety of symptoms. There are five different products in the range. First, Tixylix Cough and Cold (which contains pseudoephedrine hydrochloride, chlorphenamine maleate and pholcodine), soothes coughs, helps to clear congestion and relieves runny noses for children aged 1-10 years. For the same age range, Tixylix Chesty Cough (which contains guaifenesin) offers relief from catarrh and chesty coughs. Likewise, dry, tickly daytime coughs can be eased with Tixylix Dry Cough (which contains pholcodine).

The fourth product in the Tixylix range soothes irritating night-time coughs, again for children aged 1-10 years. It's called Tixylix Night Cough and contains promethazine hydrochloride and pholcodine. Finally, Tixylix Baby Syrup, which contains glycerol, provides soothing relief for dry coughs for babies from three months old.

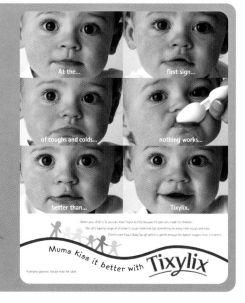

Mums kiss it better with **Tixylix**

Where would you have seen the brand?

Historically, Tixylix has built its profile and reputation by combining one of the most effective forms of communication – recommendation by word of mouth – with more traditional advertising channels.

The product has been a family medicine cabinet stalwart for generations. Tixylix is frequently recommended by mums to their friends and then eventually to their children's children.

The brand's advertising over the last 45 years has moved with the times, but has always been engaging, emotive, modern and relevant. Tixylix was first advertised on TV in 1989. The brand's most recent advertising strap line, 'Mums kiss it better with Tixylix', reflects the trust, warmth and support which the brand evokes.

Today, the brand is also promoted through a carefully targeted, integrated campaign that uses different media channels. The creative marketing is aimed at new mothers using a combination of

parenting magazines, popular 'new mum' websites and dedicated maternity initiatives such as the Bounty packs, which are distributed in hospitals to new mothers. Through these different media channels Tixylix has developed innovative campaigns to raise brand awareness and educate consumers about the brand. These include

Tixylix photo albums inserted into the Bounty packs and the sponsorship of the Mother & Baby magazine website, which provides information for young families by offering a plethora of ideas for keeping healthy children happy.

The brand also uses sponsorship to get more involved in local community initiatives and with the retailers who stock Tixylix. For five successive years, following its conception in 1998, Tixylix sponsored the high profile Child Friendly Pharmacy of the Year. This national award recognises and rewards pharmacies that play an important role in their local community and help to make busy mums' lives easier.

How was the brand developed?

Tixylix was first formulated in the UK around 45 years ago. When it was first launched, the brand was only available to consumers through a prescription from their GP. It is now available to buy direct from the pharmacy, and does not require a prescription from a doctor.

What does the brand promise you?

The success of Tixylix has been built on its strong and established reputation as a straightforward, honest brand. Parents can trust its product range to quickly soothe their children's uncomfortable symptoms of coughs and colds, such as runny or blocked noses and chesty or dry coughs. It also offers pleasant-tasting products free from sugar and colours.

Indeed, some of the products in the range, such as Tixylix Chesty Cough and Tixylix Baby Syrup, can be bought straight from a shop shelf. They are on the General Sales List, which means they can be purchased without the permission of a pharmacist, and are available from the self-selection medicine shelves in pharmacies, supermarkets or local independent shops.

Since its introduction, nearly 45 years ago, Tixylix has achieved and maintained the position of number one selling medicine for children's coughs and colds. It currently commands a 47.3% share of the market (Source: IRI HBA All Outlets 52 W/E December 24th 2005). This equates to over 2.5 million bottles of Tixylix being sold every year.

Did you know?

Learning to blow your nose is one of the hardest things for a child to achieve. To help children overcome this, Tixylix produced the first-ever guide to blowing your nose, entitled 'No More Snail Trails'. The leaflet was hugely popular, making an appearance on the daytime TV show, This Morning.

Always read the label.

Tommee Tippee has been a key player in the baby accessories market in the UK since 1965. Historically known for bright colours, innovative designs, quality and value for money, the brand was at first characterised by a little brown bear and later by a mischievous panda.

Tommee Tippee is best known for its cups and feeding products for babies. In 2005 Tommee Tippee sold more than 22 million products. This has propelled the brand to be the highest-placed baby accessories company in the top 10 performing baby care brands last year, coming in at number eight with 26% growth (Source: TNS Superpanel, The Grocer).

What is Tommee Tippee?

Although Tommee Tippee's first range focused on cups for toddlers, the brand now makes products for all stages from pregnancy onwards. Alongside feeding accessories, it also offers baby monitors, nappy wrappers, toys, soothers and teethers. On quality, the award-winning brand's range also exceeds statutory and customer requirements.

Tommee Tippee is well regarded for its focus on practical innovation. The baby products brand has one of the largest patent portfolios in its category, which alone generate 30% of annual sales. The brand has launched a number of innovations for the baby accessories market including the dentally-approved Easiflow cup, the new Magic Gripper mat and the Nappy Wrapper, a twist and seal nappy disposal system.

The range offers a wide variety of products from pre-birth through to toddler. These include a monitor with a sensor pad to pick up a baby's tiniest movements and a folding travel potty that uses disposable liners. The range offers a choice to parents whether breast or bottle feeding, using real nappies or disposables, non-spill beakers or health professional-endorsed valve-free cups. It also has a Disney baby range of products which include a baby rein, weaning spoon, shampoo shield, bottles, cups and bibs.

Where would you have seen the brand?

Tommee Tippee has more than 96% distribution through all channels including baby specialist stores, supermarkets, 3,000 independent chemists, nursery shops and department stores. Its products are stocked in well-known, high street shops such as Boots, John Lewis, Mothercare, Toys R Us, Argos and Woolworths, as well as supermarkets such as ASDA, Tesco and Sainsbury's. Internationally, the brand is sold in more than 25 countries. Its products are also available to buy through its website www.tommeetippee.com.

Tommee Tippee's 50-year experience in selling and promoting baby accessories has led to a targeted approach to marketing, promotions and sales. Its integrated approach includes targeted marketing campaigns, promotions, brand literature and retail support to drive consumer demand of its products.

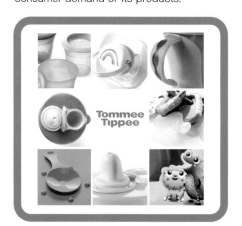

How was the brand developed?

First registered in America 50 years ago, Tommee Tippee arrived in the UK in 1965 with just 10 products, including the stay-warm bowl (mum had to pour boiling water into a hole in the base of the bowl to keep baby's food warm) and the hard plastic 'pelican' bib which is still sold today. In the early 1990s the brand dominated the market place with a range of more than 350 products.

Generations of parents have weaned their children with Tommee Tippee cups, bowls, plates, spoons and bibs. Innovation is at the heart of the brand, and Tommee Tippee has had a number of 'firsts'.

In the 1980s, Tommee Tippee broke new ground by being the first to launch a non-spill cup – the Sip 'n' Seal cup. It also

What does the brand promise you?

With a range stretching from pregnancy to toddler, Tommee Tippee aims to bring mothers the best and easiest solutions to everyday parenting choices. Tommee Tippee believes babies love the products and that's why parents recommend them.

Did you know?

pioneered the first Heat Sensor range for babies with a thermochromic material that changes colour when food or drinks is too hot to be consumed safely. This is a concept that was endorsed by the Child Accident Prevention Trust and showcased in the Millennium Dome.

Tommee Tippee was also the first brand to use primary colours in feeding products – its lime green, orange and yellow range five years ago revolutionised the children's tableware section in store.

It was also the first baby brand to win the support of the British Dental Health Foundation for Easiflow, a non-spill cup which works without a valve, thus reducing the dental problems that may arise in babies and toddlers from regular use of valved cups.

Other significant successes include The Nappy Wrapper, number one in every country it is sold in. This is a patented twist and seal disposal system for disposable nappies, ensuring nappy changing with no smells, germs and mess. The Tommee Tippee Steri-bottle, the world's first fully disposable, fully recyclable feeding bottle, has also been a great success.

The 2006 range includes a stay-clean spoon and a gripper mat which stops babies from throwing their plates to the floor while helping them feed successfully. Other launches in 2006 include the Closer to Nature breastfeeding support range with a revolutionary teat that helps babies to breastfeed for longer. Tommee Tippee is also the biggest brand to enter the growing real nappy market with Cotton Bottoms.

In today's environment, rising concerns of the increase in child obesity means parents are painstakingly aware of ensuring their children have healthy, active lifestyles. Similarly, studies by educational psychologists suggest that children become more skilful if they're physically fit while young.

Tumble Tots preceded recent trends when it was launched in 1979 with a focus on healthy living for kids. Its mobile, active programme has been designed to help children with their physical and social development.

What is Tumble Tots?

The Tumble Tots programme caters for five different age groups of children ranging from six months to seven years-old. Members attend a weekly session where they participate in a variety of activities to develop their physical and social skills, while songs and rhymes help their language development.

The 40 minute Gymbabes classes are for babies of six months to toddlers who can walk; there are a further three 45 minute Tumble Tots programmes catering for different ages – from walking to two years, two to three years and three years to school age. Finally, the 50 minute Gymbobs classes are for children of school age to seven years-old.

The children learn physical skills by using specially-developed, brightly-coloured wooden and foam Tumble Tots equipment such as bars, trestles, balance boards, ladders, balls and hoops. The tasks differ according to their age group and stage of development, allowing children to develop at their own pace.

In addition, the brand has recently launched Leaps and Bounds, a movement and physical development programme to cater for the increasing number of toddlers attending nurseries.

Physical activity for pre-school children is a niche market within the growing childcare sector and Tumble Tots is the market leader, as the only national provider of active physical play for this age group.

Where would you have seen the brand?

Since its launch Tumble Tots has grown to become a well-established national and international children's brand. In the UK there are over 500 centres operated by more than 100 franchisees with 60,000 Tumble Tot members. The brand organises and co-ordinates advertising, promotional and PR activities on a national basis, assisted by Tumble Tots' Franchisees who market their business locally.

Tumble Tots advertising appears in national parenting magazines to build awareness of the brand. National promotional campaigns also play an important role and they are often organised in conjunction with household brand names. Pampers, Huggies, Müller, Keycamp,

Legoland Windsor, Bob the Builder and Noddy are just some of the brands who have or continue to work with Tumble Tots.

Tumble Tots uses national PR campaigns that also serve as a brand building tool. In February, the brand runs a healthy eating campaign called Eat Fit Keep Fit, in May, Positive Parenting focuses on parenting issues and in October, National Children's Activity Week inspires parents with ideas to get their children involved in physical activities.

Additionally, the brand organises a biennial fundraising activity, which has donated to charities including the Great Ormond Street Hospital, BBC Children In Need, Action Research and the NSPCC. Individual Tumble Tots Franchisees also organise their own campaigns for local charities.

The Tumble Tots website plays an important role. It includes a search facility to identify local centres, useful parenting information, a chat room, activities for children and an online shop.

How was the brand developed?

Tumble Tots was established in 1979 by Bill Cosgrave, who was a coach for the 1968 British Olympic Gymnastics team. Bill began his professional coaching career in the Army Physical Training Corp, where he spent six years. After his Olympics training experience, he became a gymnastics coach with the Southampton Education Authority.

While in Southampton, Bill realised that school children were struggling to learn gymnastics through their PE classes, as they lacked basic motor skills. This revelation led Bill to introduce the Physical Skills Award structure in schools, and to launch the Southampton Gymnastics Club. He extended the programme to cater for pre-school children, which led to the birth of the Tumble Tots concept with its specially designed equipment.

The value of Tumble Tots is backed up by specialist senior educational psychologist and author Madeleine Portwood who says she would recommend it to parents concerned about a child experiencing difficulties with the acquisition of motor skills. She believes the sessions are well structured, run by trained staff and designed to benefit all children under seven.

In 1990, Tumble Tots in the UK acquired one of the leading British parenting magazines 'Right Start'. Today this is distributed bi-monthly to Tumble Tots members and is also available on some newsstands. The brand has also extended into a range of action song DVDs, CDs and a home exercise DVD programme.

What does the brand promise you?

Twenty six years on, Tumble Tots is trusted and recognised as the UK's leading brand in pre-school children's physical play with 60,000 attending members. Its commitment to developing children's physical skills and boosting their self-confidence, independence, self-discipline, self-worth and sense of security and identity is the brand's driving force.

The brand has and will continue to encourage parents and children to lead a healthy lifestyle. By nurturing children's enjoyment of physical activity from a young age the brand will maintain its commitment to building a healthier future.

Did you know?

Since its launch in 1979, more than a million children worldwide have benefited from the Tumble Tots programme.

Studies by educational psychologists show that a child's skills are enhanced if their levels of self-confidence, physical fitness and motor control are raised during the early formative and elementary years.

Sally Gunnell, Olympic Gold medallist and TV presenter, is a firm believer in the Tumble Tots brand. Her sons have been through the Tumble Tots programme.

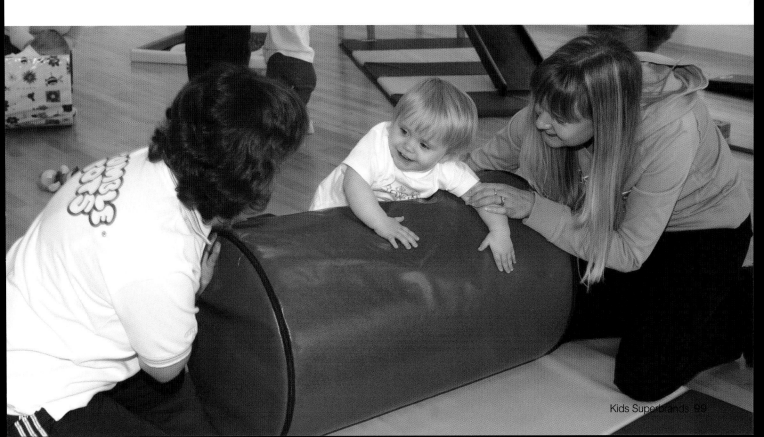

Venture has transformed the neglected category of portrait photography into a contemporary art form. It is a progressive brand that has revolutionised a tired, forgotten, low-value category that had changed little in over 150 years.

Before Venture's launch, portrait photography was characterised by stiff, lifeless, posed portraits and was largely rejected by modern consumers. The sector was populated by local independent studios, lacked leadership and had no big brands.

What is Venture?

Venture is a product, service and experience, all rolled into one brand. Its core target is families with children. It offers them a vehicle for self-expression that 'captures the real you' and dramatises individuality.

It is a brand that taps into key contemporary trends such as personalisation and customisation. Consumers today, want more than a standard family portrait in their living space. They want to be able to adapt and transform the art in their homes so that it becomes more personal and meaningful.

Venture doesn't just 'do portraits', but aims to tell stories that celebrate life and relationships. That's why the brand's strap line is, 'Every Venture Tells A Story'.

The brand has a team of talented photographers, designers and interiors experts to create contemporary portraiture and transform family images into modern icons. The brand demands creative excellence at all stages of the process and uses advanced digital processes to deliver the final results.

With over 80 studios all over the UK, the brand experience for families begins with a one-hour, fun-filled studio session to capture the initial images. An extensive product range of hand-crafted displays enables clients to transform these images into personal pieces of contemporary art for their homes.

every
venture
tells
a story

Where would you have seen the brand?

Venture advertises nationwide and also invests in PR. Press ads and inserts appear regularly in glossy, monthly women's magazines, home interest and parenting titles as well as newspaper weekend supplements.

Venture's website (www.thisisventure.co.uk) is an essential marketing channel. It is visited by an average of 50,000 people every month.

Venture also uses exhibition stands at major retail outlets as a marketing channel to attract busy consumers: this sees Venture tour shopping malls around the UK, as well as major centres like Bluewater and The Trafford Centre.

Word-of-mouth and recommendation play a vital role in building the brand's profile. Many first experience Venture by attending a 'Venture At Home' party, held by new

customers to show their friends and family the new portraits in their home, in a relaxed environment, where they can benefit from special referral offers.

More recently Venture has launched its 'Creative Adventure Portrait Experience' which is distributed through retailers such as Boots, Tesco, Debenhams and Harrods: this promotional pack contains all the information a customer needs to commission their very own New Generation Portrait.

What does the brand promise you?

The brand's strap line 'Every Venture Tells A Story' captures its central promise, which is to provide customers with a symbol of 'the real you', expressed through the notion of storytelling. Aspirational values underpin the brand's ability to transform the ordinary portrait into an art form.

How was the brand developed?

Brian Glover-Smith, the founder and CEO of Venture, began his career as a photographer in 1976. During this time he gained many professional accolades including a number of important national and international photography awards. Glover-Smith is a winner of six Kodak European Gold Awards and the Kodak European Photographer of the Year Award. He is also a Fellow of the Chartered Institute of Marketing.

Disillusioned with traditional portrait photography, Glover-Smith and a team of like-minded pioneers launched Venture as a franchise business with backing from Kodak, opening the first gallery-style studios in 2000.

The brand's ambition is to become a global leader in the consumer photographic products market, and Venture studios in Hong Kong and Miami are set for launch in early 2006.

Photography innovation is at the heart of Venture's business, and the brand both encourages its employees to continually strive to improve, and also places an emphasis on new product development.

Did you know?

Celebrities, including champion jockey Frankie Dettori, swimmer and TV presenter Sharon Davies, footballer Rio Ferdinand, TV and radio presenters Lorraine Kelly and Jo Whiley, as well as Angela Griffin and Peter Schmeichel, have all had a Venture.

A recent research study supported psychologists' theory that positive images of the family on display in the home benefit the emotional health and confidence of children.

Aside from families, other subject matter that Venture has photographed includes pet dogs, cats, goats, snakes, and even a tame sheep.

VERTBAUDET

Putting children first...™

www.vertbaudet.co.uk

VERTBAUDET, the kid's clothing specialist, provides colourful, continental baby and childrenswear in the UK. The brand is well-established in France where it is now the market leader in clothing for the under nines. It launched its UK home shopping service in 1997 and has become a firm favourite for busy parents looking for functional and appealing children's fashion.

VERTBAUDET's products are showcased in two catalogues, a 242 page fashion collection and a 52 page home brochure, which are sent out twice a year. These catalogues and its website www.vertbaudet.co.uk attract over 550,000 customers.

What is VERTBAUDET?

VERTBAUDET offers an extensive collection of clothing and footwear for mothers-to-be, infants and children aged up to 12 through its catalogues and website. Its fashion collections are filled with fun clothing created by the brand's stylists alongside special-edition collections developed by designers such as Katherine Roumanoff.

Although French in origin, VERTBAUDET is an international retailer. Following success in the UK market, it rolled out its home shopping service into Portugal in 1999 and Spain in 2005. In its home market of France it also has a network of 23 high street stores.

Where would you have seen the brand?

Aside from its catalogues, VERTBAUDET has a very popular website which had over four million visitors last year. It has more than 1,400 items available online with interactive catalogues, where customers can flick through the pages and click on items of interest. Telephone customer service advisers are also on hand seven days a week to deal with customer queries.

VERTBAUDET uses a broad range of channels to recruit customers – including advertising in leading baby magazines, maternity sample programmes and mailing mini-catalogues.

VERTBAUDET's innovative approach has been endorsed with a steady stream of awards. They include the number one mail order catalogue for baby & childrenswear under nine by GfK from 1999-2005, and for toys & nursery from 2004-2005.

Other awards include the Prima Baby reader awards, mail order category for both 'Best Buy' and 'Best Value' in 2004/05 and Tommy's Parent Friendly Awards nominated for Best Home Shopping Retailer and Best Premature Range in 2003/04.

How was the brand developed?

VERTBAUDET was launched in France in the mid 1960s. In 1997, it spotted a gap in the UK market for kids clothing. UK mothers wanted something a little different. They wanted practical, well-priced children's clothing, but they wanted it to come with more style.

VERTBAUDET is owned by Redcats which employs over 2,000 people in the

UK, and is part of PPR, one of Europe's leading retail groups and number three in the luxury goods sector worldwide.

From day one, even the tiniest of premature babies are catered for with a special newborn range starting from just 2.5 kilos. Designed alongside medical staff, this unique collection is made from soft fabric and features accessible front openings for when the baby needs special care and attention. Colin Colline also caters for babies of up to 24 months and provides everything for the new arrival, including items for the nursery.

Additionally, the best-selling O'Kids ranges offers cute, colourful clothing for toddlers, while the bohemian chic of Mila Blue includes special-occasion wear in rich fabrics for parties, weddings, christenings and family-get-togethers.

The brand is continually diversifying and innovating. For example, in 2003 it launched a home collection for the UK market, which features bedding, furnishings, accessories for children's rooms and toys. And as part of its 'Putting children first' ethos, the brand ran a contest for budding furniture designers and featured the winning designs in its Spring/Summer 2006 catalogue.

What does the brand promise you?

For UK mothers with children aged 0-12, VERTBAUDET is the brand which offers the widest range of children's clothing with a distinctive style, combining fun, quality and practicality. VERTBAUDET always puts children first and offers children and mothers something original, different and distinctive French designs, which stand out from the ubiquity of UK high street fashion.

VERTBAUDET products also represent excellent value for money. The children's clothing is meticulously tested for colour fastness, tear-resistance and repeated washing. VERTBAUDET's clothes use high quality, practical, easy-care fabrics to make them more suitable for kids. They include clever details such as zips, press studs, elasticised waistbands and adjustable leg lengths.

The clothing is designed to make it easier for kids to put on themselves. Wide collars,

Velcro fastenings and elastic finishing touches make getting dressed in the morning easy for the kids, and means minimum fuss for the whole family on hectic weekday mornings.

VERTBAUDET's determination to put children first also means the brand has a strong sense of fun. Aside from being practical, the clothes also have fun designs and inventive choices of colour. This combination of practicality and fun also extends into the new home collection, especially with the storage solutions.

VERTBAUDET appreciates the importance of providing a convenient service for young families. It's especially true for new mothers who want to avoid the hassle of lugging a pushchair around the shops in a busy town. Instead, VERTBAUDET offers delivery of its products direct to its customers' homes, with any unwanted items returned free of charge.

Did you know?

VERTBAUDET translates from French as 'Green Donkey'.

In 2006, VERTBAUDET designed an organic baby range in hypo-allergenic cotton to protect baby's sensitive skin.

A proportion of the sales of the VERTBAUDET premature range are donated to Tommy's the baby charity.

In 2005 VERTBAUDET had more than four million visitors to its website.

VERTBAUDET ships more than 5.4 million packages annually.

VTech specialises in developing learning toys for children between the ages of 0-10 years. The global brand has also pioneered and created the electronic learning products (ELP) category and has grown to become a highly regarded and trusted consumer brand.

Since 1976, VTech has been developing high-quality, innovative educational toys. The toys combine entertaining, curriculum-based, learning content, including melodies and friendly voiced out instructions. VTech is a brand that advocates 'smart play', so that children can learn while having fun.

What is VTech?

VTech has many different product categories, which are detailed below.

V.Smile was launched in 2004 and fast became one of the top five selling toys (Source: NPD). This award-winning pre-school system, combining a balance of fun and learning, is available in a console that can be played at home through the TV. A portable version was launched in 2005, which can be played 'on the go'. V.Smile has a library of over 30 different learning games, featuring a wide variety of well-known licensed characters.

New to VTech's portfolio is V.Smile Baby, an infant development system for babies aged 9-36 months. The product has three different modes of play to cater for babies as they grow, so that they can watch, learn and interact with their mums to learn fundamentals such as colours, shapes and objects.

V.Flash is a product that expands on the success and values of V.Smile. It is a CD-based learning system for kids aged six years and older. V.Flash has 3D video

game graphics with three sections to each title, 'edugaming', learning and creativity to deliver a balance of education and entertainment. A library of learning games is available using characters from the small screen to cinema to enhance the learning experience.

For older children, VTech has a series of electronic learning computers, which are pre-loaded with a variety of age-appropriate curriculum related programmes. A user-friendly interface and spoken instructions enable children to grasp school subjects in a fun and engaging way. The electronic learning computers also have many features including stereo sound, foreign languages, typing tutors and parent progress reports.

VTech has a range of interactive learning toys targeted towards pre-school

children. They teach pre-school essentials such as phonics, letters, numbers, spelling and letter writing. VTech uses technologies in its range such as letter recognition to help children learn cursive writing to enhance their development. The VTech Pre-School range aims to help children prepare for starting school so that they can progress confidently through their first years of structured learning.

The VTech Baby range has been designed to bring out the best in babies, infants and toddlers, by encouraging them to play, learn and discover. These toys stimulate children's senses and imagination by combining play with talking, interaction, bright buttons and flashing lights. They also offer age-appropriate concepts such as letters, numbers, shapes, colours and objects. More recently, SmartVille has been introduced, which is a range of interactive, imaginative play sets enhanced with smart technology, featuring popular scenes and a host of characters.

Additionally, VTech has a number of interactive toys that tap into children's love of cartoon and film characters. Taking a VTech pre-school laptop and adding popular children's characters such as Winnie the Pooh, enhances a child's learning experience. As well as the pre-school laptops, VTech has developed a wide variety of learning toys featuring Winnie the Pooh, Dora the Explorer, Bob the Builder and Disney Princess. Each toy combines VTech technology with hands-on play to stimulate children's imagination while teaching colours, shapes, letters, numbers, spelling, objects and music.

Where would you have seen the brand?

VTech has 100% distribution in the UK toy market. Its products are available through all toy retailers, department stores, supermarkets, mail order and online. In 2005, VTech was positioned as the fifth largest group in the total toy market (Source: NPD).

VTech takes a dual approach to its marketing. While 85% of its brand-building strategy targets parents, 15% of its advertising targets children. VTech markets its brand through a variety of different channels which includes TV advertising, press, direct mail, PR and product placement, as well as point of sale within retail and trade exhibitions. VTech also appears at The Baby Show. Its two websites www.vtechuk.com and www.vsmile.co.uk also provide an essential marketing channel.

VTech's products have won numerous awards. The brand was most recently awarded 'Toy Supplier of the Year' by the British Association of Toy Retailers. In addition, V.Smile, the pre-school video gaming and learning console, received the Electronic Learning Toy of the Year from the British Association of Toy Retailers in 2004.

How was the brand developed?

VTech was launched in 1976 and launched in the UK in 1988. However, its products have been distributed in the UK since the early 1980s by Adam Leisure under the Grandstand brand, which predominantly sold electronic learning computers. The products made by VTech were the 'Small Talk Pre-school Telephone' and the 'Pre-school Computer 1000'. In 1991 VTech (UK) floated on the stock exchange, which led to further product investment and VTech's establishment of an electronic learning category.

Did you know?

VTech is a US$2 billion brand specialising in electronic learning toys and telecommunications.

VTech's a virtually integrated manufacturer with a factory based in China which stretches over one million square foot.

The VTech brand has 85% recall from parents with children aged from birth to eight years (Source: LVQ).

What does the brand promise you?

VTech's brand statement is simple: 'We take play patterns that children love and create clever toys by adding technology and curriculum.' This is echoed in the brand's strap line: 'Very interactive…Very clever…Very VTech!'

Brand Guardians

Bambino Mio

Guy Schanschieff
Managing Director

Guy graduated from De Montfort University, Leicester in 1989, with a BA Hons Business Studies degree. He demonstrated his leadership qualities early in his career when, during his teens he formed a Theatre Production Company with friends, taking their successful production to the Edinburgh Fringe Festival. Guy and his wife, Jo have three children and there first hand experience in parenting has been the driving force behind the Bambino Mio brand strategy. As Founder and Chairman of the Nappy Alliance, in 2003, Guy is actively involved in Government lobbying in support of reusable nappies.

Bounty

Simon Williamson
Managing Director

Simon spent his early years at Publicis and D'Arcy's, working on brands such as Renault, Halfords, Bisto and Tetley Tea, before joining Bounty in 1992. Simon joined the Board in 1997, and became Managing Director of Bounty in 2002.

He led the management buy out in late 2004 and is immensely proud of what Bounty stands for. Simon is passionate about Bounty's role in becoming "experts in everyday family life" and providing trusted information, support and a range of value added services.

Husband and father of two, Simon believes that business success is driven by marketing and insight. For Bounty this is of course about families being at the heart of its culture.

Britax

Paul Brindley
Marketing Director,
Europe

After gaining postgraduate marketing qualifications, Paul, spent 15 years in a variety of fields including sales, distribution, finance and manufacturing. He has been a key figure in marketing and brand management with companies such as Pentland, Unilever, Energizer and Spillers. Before joining Britax in Spring 2005, Paul spent time working in Hungary, Poland, Czech, Russia and Switzerland.

Paul Scott Fleming
Managing Director,
Europe

After graduating from Salford University, Paul started his career with Rover who sponsored his studies. He spent 10 years working in the safety field before moving into sales, marketing and then general management, working for blue chip companies such as Jaguar, TRW and Volkswagen. Paul was President of Volkswagon in Brazil before joining Britax in mid 2004.

British Airways London Eye

Jo Berrington
Head of Marketing

Jo trained at Leeds in design, photography and printing. She joined the London Eye team on secondment from British Airways in November 2000 to take up the unique challenge as Head of Marketing, with the responsibility of driving an average of 3.8 million visitors to the attraction a year. Jo worked closely with Andrew Mulholland of Futurebrand to develop a brand positioning, which now drives all marketing communications activity and enables the team at the London Eye to harness and nurture their passion for the brand and deliver a business benefit.

Caboodle Bags

Ruth Kirby-Smith
Founder

Ruth was a busy academic, running a large research contract when she had her first child, Julia. Frustrated with the lack of bags/holdalls to carry the essential pieces of baby equipment, Ruth set on designing her perfect bag to carry nappies, food, clean clothes, wipes and lotions, in fact the whole Caboodle!

Almost 20 years later Ruth is still designing Caboodle Bags and is proud of the company ethos, which has been flexible enough to allow employees to work for Caboodle and bring up their families. Ruth is also proud of the reputation established with mothers and within the nursery industry for quality, service and reliability, all provided at a fair price.

CASIO®

Hiroshi Fujii
Managing Director

Hiroshi has been with the CASIO Corporation for 24 years, becoming Managing Director of CASIO UK in January 2003. Hiroshi has been crucial to the success of the company, taking a hands-on approach to ensure that the CASIO brand continually inspires passion. Hiroshi sees his role as an opportunity to focus on the specific needs of customers within the UK, whilst committing to the philosophy of Creativity and Contribution.

David Hodgkinson
Brand Communications
Manager

David joined CASIO seven years ago working in Brand Marketing with the G-Shock brand. Since then he has overseen the launch of CASIO's Exilim digital cameras into the UK & Eire markets, and latterly has been responsible for the implementation of the CASIOLOGY campaign, designed to challenge and alter consumer perceptions.

Eurocamp

Deborah Beckett
Managing Director

As Managing Director of Eurocamp, Deborah is responsible for directing all brand activity across the company's six operating countries including the UK, the Netherlands, Germany, Denmark, Poland and Switzerland.

Deborah looks after every aspect of the Eurocamp brand, including communication strategies such as the recent television advertising campaign and ensuring the brand has a continuous programme of innovative product development.

Day-to-day, Deborah ensures the Eurocamping experience – from the quality of accommodation to the wide range of free children's clubs – meets the high standards you'd expect from the leading tour operator for European holidays in mobile homes and tents.

grobag®

Rob Holmes
Managing Director

Rob, 36, is the Co-Creator of the award-winning grobag® baby sleeping bags and Managing Director of gro-group™ International, a company that specialises in providing practical nursery products. At the same time, he manages a busy nightclub in South Devon.

Rob's rise within the nursery sector has been relatively fast, following the birth of his first son Samuel, which led him and his wife, Ouvrielle, to develop grobag baby sleeping bags as a safe alternative to sheets and blankets.

Rob is passionate about the grobag brand and was responsible for developing the launch campaign that has contributed to the brand's phenomenal success.

Haliborange

Fiona Walkley
UK & International
Marketing Manager

Fiona grew up on Haliborange and loves being custodian for one of the best known, most trusted children's brands. The Healthcare sector is one of the most dynamic categories around. Fiona has been a part of Seven Seas Ltd's successful marketing team for nine years and together they share a passion for making a positive contribution to consumers' health.

Milkshake!

Nick Wilson
Controller of Children's
Programming

Nick is one of British television's most experienced children's TV executives whose career has spanned over 30 years. He joined Five as Controller of Children's Programmes in March 1996, since then, Nick and his team have masterminded the rapid rise and continued success of the Milkshake! brand. His ability to see the potential for a successful programme, alongside his direct and engaging presenters and consistent scheduling, has ensured Milkshake! is a safe, successful, entertaining and engaging pre-school brand.

Practical Parenting

Mara Lee
Editor

Mara has been Editor of Practical Parenting in the UK since June 2004. Prior to this she was Editor of Practical Parenting in Australia, during which time she also wrote two parenting books, Baby's First Year for Dummies and Staying Mum: The First Year, both published by John Wiley & Associates in Australia. She has two children, Jayna, aged seven and Cooper aged five.

Ilka Schmitt
Publisher

Ilka has published Practical Parenting since March 2005. She has worked at IPC for eight years in a variety of IPC divisions most recently as a Publisher in IPC's specialist magazine division, IPC Country & Leisure, publishing six specialist titles.

Sylvanian Families

Peter Brown
CEO

Peter is CEO and Co-Founder of Flair plc, the award winning Toy Company and distributor of Sylvanian Families. Peter first saw Sylvanian Families in 1985. He was immediately captivated by the family values and wholesome play that the concept portrays. Peter has strived to ensure the enduring appeal continues as the product approaches its 20th anniversary in the UK.

Simon Harwood
Partner SSK Productions

Simon has worked on Sylvanian Families marketing and advertising since its UK launch in 1987. During that time he has also designed and modelled three of the families and five structures. He launched the Sylvanian Token Scheme and still runs the club as well as the Sylvanian Shop and a large Sylvanian mail order/internet business.

Venture

Brian Glover-Smith
CEO

Brian launched Venture as a franchise business, opening the first gallery style studios in 2000. As CEO and Founder, Brian has managed Venture's growth to its current position as the leading portrait brand in the UK. He is a winner of six Kodak European Gold Awards and the coveted title of European Photographer of the Year Award, Brian is also a fellow of the Chartered Institute of Marketing.

Chris Pass
Head of Marketing

Chris was appointed to lead the development and execution of the Venture brand and marketing strategy in 2004. Previously with Boots Healthcare International and United Biscuits, Chris joined Venture with a wealth of strategic, international and operational marketing experience gained across a range of brands including Clearasil, Strepsils and McVitie's Penguin.

VERTBAUDET

Steve Parkes
UK General Manager

As head of the UK team Steve works closely with his colleagues in France to adapt the VERTBAUDET offer and develop the UK market share. Steve feels the key to his success is having a great brand to manage, an excellent product to offer and a strong, clear positioning in the market. With end customers that are children, a sense of fun is maintained in the team! Prior to leading VERTBAUDET, Steve used his marketing skills to launch La Redoute in the UK. Alongside developing VERTBAUDET's market share of the web, Steve's next priority is to develop partnerships in the baby and children's universe.

The Power of Playtime
By Jacqueline Harding & Dr Sanjay Chaudhuri

Help your child grow up with the best possible chance of health, happiness and success

'Tomorrow's Child' works with companies to enable them to equip children for the future. Director Jacqueline Harding, who is also Education Editor for the BBC & Dr Sanjay Chaudhuri, Medical Director of 'Tomorrow's Child' share their Top Ten Play Tips.

Despite overwhelming evidence, the value of play is still massively underestimated by most people. In order to help children have the greatest chance of health, happiness and educational success, children need to play.

In the next three minutes you will learn the true value of play, how to play for the greatest success and where to acquire the best play habits and tools. This will ensure an incredible relationship with your child as he or she grows up to become a successful playful adult.

The True Value of Play

The effects of play go far beyond the notion of simply keeping children (and adults) occupied. In fact, educational research shows that play is nature's well kept secret, a high performance learning tool.

Here are the six most important benefits of play:

- Builds self-esteem and confidence
- Accelerates learning and academic performance
- Helps navigate the world's challenges
- Creates better health
- Stimulates brain development
- Develops social skills

Unfortunately most people don't understand the power of play as an educational model and most adults have forgotten how to play effectively.

However, this is readily remedied with our 10 top tips for 'Tomorrows Child'.

How to Play - Ten Top Tips

1. Feed Your Child's Brain with Play
Play is essential as it literally feeds the brain. The developing brains of children are designed for play – the neurons happily buzz around making the all-important synaptic connections as conversations take place between the right and left hand side of the brain. All in all, the brain gets busy lapping up the lively stimulation created through play.

'The brain is like a muscle. When it is in use we feel very good. Understanding is joyous.' Carl Sagan

In other words your child needs time to play.

2. Give Your Child Three Daily Portions of Play
Avoid play malnourishment! The International Play Association advises three portions of play a day as a 'healthy diet' for the brain. Here at Tomorrow's Child, we see that this is a great prescription and will encourage a child's nervous systems to mature, develop and function optimally.

There are three main basic types of play, a bit like the three major food groups:

- Active Physical Play
- Creativity and Imaginative Play
- Curiosity, Discovery and Exploration Play

Active – Physical Play
This type of play is usually energetic and helps your child to explore the possibilities and limitations of their body. It involves developing those fine movements that prepare them for pencil control and large movements that allow them to run and jump.

Playing outdoors is not only totally refreshing for your child but essential as it allows the brain to obtain the oxygen it needs.

Creativity and Imaginative Play

Creativity is about making new connections, new ways of seeing and perceiving the world. Creativity is a uniquely personal and deeply satisfying experience and closely linked to emotional expression and feelings of safety and self-worth.

Needless to say, it is fundamental to successful learning. Being creative enables children to make connections between one area of learning and another and so extend their learning.

It's worth knowing that whilst your child is engaging in fantasy and imaginative play they are paving the way ahead for the development of problem solving skills – one of the most essential of all life-skills.

Curiosity, Discovery and Exploration Play

Children often have their best ideas and greatest revelations, whilst playing. Just watch their faces, the expressions tell all – the motivation is present; the awe and wonder of the world is expressed in their every move; they are on their tip toes, ready to explode with curiosity (which, of course, fuels learning – in a significant way). Play brings out the vibrancy of life itself.

3. Positive Attention and Being a Great 'Play Companion'

Your child's nervous system thrives on positive attention. When children say 'Watch me!' they need someone close to them to appreciate their accomplishments – be it a handstand, a drawing or a new model made out of clay. No wonder play builds self-esteem – it's a way of affirming who you are.

Being a play companion will help them 'feel strong on the inside', ready for whatever comes their way in life. So, don't forget to give yourself permission to have fun and be child-like.

In order to play, children need a supportive, nurturing, stimulating atmosphere where the brain feels alive, alert to new possibilities.

Supportive and interested adults make invaluable companions. Children love to know someone is listening to them and valuing their contributions. Play is a very personal experience and can only be

shared on the child's terms – rightly so, as it is the creation of their mind and their ideas.

- Be curious yourself – remember what it feels like to stop and wonder at the world.
- When invited to join in play with your child, enjoy the experience.
- Show delight at every response your child makes whilst playing.

The purpose of being a good play companion is creating good play memories that last a lifetime.

4. Let's Pretend…

'Imagination will often carry us to worlds that never were. But without it we go nowhere.' **Carl Sagan**

It's important to play along with your child's imagination through 'let's pretend' games. Children create situations to play (even when resources are limited); they assume roles, rearrange the space around them and make props virtually out of nothing to assist them in their play. This way their pretend play can become three dimensional; it can come alive. There is a growing body of evidence supporting the many connections between intellectual ability and high quality pretend play.

This kind of play is an important facilitator of perspective taking and later abstract thought; it may facilitate higher-level thinking skills, and there are clear links between pretend play and social and linguistic competence.

If children are prevented from experiencing these types of play opportunities, their long-term capacities related to big picture thinking, problem solving and social awareness, as well as to academic skills such as literacy, mathematics and science, may be diminished.

These complex and multidimensional skills involving many areas of the brain are most likely to thrive in an atmosphere rich in high quality pretend play.

5. Get Creative

Creative play offers a window into their world and it's interesting to look at your child's artwork or other play materials that have malleable properties, as they can offer insight into the way your child is thinking or feeling and can tell you what is important to them.

There is no doubt that encouraging a child to get creative is often deeply satisfying. The actual act of being creative involves us all – child and adult – in a unique way as it meets our deepest needs:

- It is fulfilling mentally as it involves different thinking patterns – ones that are imaginative – out of the box and fresh.
- It can involve us physically by challenging us to use new skills and perhaps try out new creative techniques.
- It engages our emotions by compelling us to 'feel' the chosen material and to express deep emotions.

The development of creativity in a young child's life is fundamental to future effective learning. Creative play helps children build bridges that start from their individual fund of knowledge over to new pastures of knowledge.

'If you want to be creative, stay in part a child, with the creativity and invention that characterises children before they are deformed by adult society.' **Jean Piaget**

The Benefits of Creative Play:

- Allows for expression of emotions.
- Has no particular outcome dictated by adults and therefore can be truly enriching.
- Can be therapeutic often allowing children to come to terms with confusing and conflicting experiences in their lives.

6. Preparing for Creative Play

A trip to the library to look though inspiring books on drama, music, photography, fine art, sculpture etc can be a good place to start at any age. Why not keep a scrap book containing a few creative ideas to inspire your child?

The following is a suggested list of creative activities which can be adapted and used for a large age-range (of course, little ones need to be supervised constantly for safety and provided with appropriate support):

- Photography – digital cameras can make this a real possibility now at low cost.
- Using suitable creative software packages
- Making puppets
- Making puppet theatres
- Making crystals
- Recording own music
- Making moving models
- Printing/stamping
- Decoupage
- Making badges
- Making jewellery
- Woodwork
- Plaster modelling
- Making paper – from scratch

7. Get Messy! Clean Up Tips

Keeping the mess under control is always a challenge – here are a few tips.

Keep a small cardboard box in the corner of a room into which you gradually build up a store of materials, such as small cereal boxes, used cake holders, sticky tape, safe scissors and glue, small pieces of a variety of materials and, in fact, anything that is recyclable and safe.

Also, keep handy:

- A large piece of plastic sheeting that can be placed under the child and their work of art in the making.
- A shelf covered in newspaper, for new creations to dry and be admired.

- Child wipes for a quick clean-up following the burst of creativity.
- A dustpan and brush strategically placed for your child to restore order to the room.

8. Look After Yourself

We all need time to rest and nurture ourselves. The better we look after ourselves as adults, the more effective we become in nurturing creativity in our children. Here's some great advice:

- Do something creative every day of your life.
- Play in a way that makes you feel you are in a timeless zone.
- Play so that your brain feels alert to new possibilities and feels energised.

'The most dynamic people are daring originals who enjoy pushing the boundaries to break new ground.'
Marianne Velvart (Author and Singer)

9. Value the Time

It's essential to provide a safe, loving, and encouraging atmosphere with clear limits in order that children can build on past successes and continue playing into a successful and happy adulthood.

Quite simply, the quality of play your child experiences will depend upon accepting children as they are and allowing them to be who they were born to be.

10. Get the Play Habit – Playing for Life

'We do not stop playing because we grow old. We grow old because we stop playing.' **Anon**

One of the best ways to help your child develop positive self-esteem (a good sense of who they are – to feel special and to believe in themselves) is to take an active interest in their play.

We play games the way we live life. The better your child is at playing games and having fun, the more likely they are to be happy, healthy, fun loving successful sons and daughters, who possess a certain type of magic that truly helps create a wonderful life. So have fun and get playing!

Your child of tomorrow deserves it.

Tomorrow's Child is the only business consultancy that focuses on the needs of digital child in the area of media, marketing, child health and education.

www.tomorrowschild.co.uk

Trends in the Children's Market
By Barbie Clarke Managing Director Family Kids and Youth

Introduction

My look at children's trends is influenced by several factors. In running Family Kids and Youth, a market research company that looks at the family and child's market, and as Editor of 'Young Consumers', a journal that looks at new trends around the world, I'm continually monitoring both social and fashion trends. I'm also a trained psycho-dynamic therapist; I have worked with young offenders, and with children in schools, and currently I work each week as a counsellor with teenagers in Tower Hamlets, London.

It is interesting that marketing to children is under the spotlight, and children's needs are being put first. Increasingly children are being protected, and their opinions are being sought about their treatment, and what is happening to them. The UN Convention on the Rights of the Child led to an act being passed the UK in 1989 that for the first time gave significant recognition to the individuality of the child over and above both their parents and the state. In 2004 The Children's Act was passed, opening the door for the appointment of a Children's Commissioner in England. Professor Al Aynsley-Green

FamilyKiDSandYouth.com

and his colleagues at the Commission had to be interviewed by a panel of 25 children from the Children's Youth Board before the job was theirs.

I'm going to consider three themes: the way in which children are beginning to take a keen interest in their world; the impact of technology on children's lives; and the change to children's diet and activity levels brought about by increasing levels of childhood obesity.

The Pre-'Whatever' Generation

Children will increasingly become involved in measures that help the world: to stem global warming, to support free trade, and to respect others, in their family, and at school.

We live in extraordinary times, with today's grandparents, those of the Baby Boom generation, refusing to grow up. We hear stories of people of 60+ going on a 'gap year', or just continually on holiday. Alongside that we have the 'SKI' phenomenon (Spending Kids' Inheritance). We have witnessed the boom in gym membership, ever increasing beauty and spa treatments, and even plastic surgery, all in a quest not to grow old. Age groups are increasingly indistinguishable, visiting the same retail outlets, wearing the same clothes. And we have to ask, if adults refuse to grow up, how can children remain young? There has been a phrase in marketing banded about for some years now known as 'KGOY' (Kids Growing Older Younger). So it is increasingly difficult to define childhood, and it is difficult for children to

remain young. But children are of course just that; they are young, and their needs must be considered. We are all familiar with adolescents, and indeed probably remember that time vividly, a time well depicted by Harry Enfield's 'Kevin', and a couple of years ago Liam Lynch: dissolute, disaffected, disinterested youth 'United States of Whatever'.

But what about children before they reach that age, what is happening in their world? Our research shows that today's children (and I'll define that as under 12), actually mock the 'Whatever' attitude; they do not want to be teenagers, even describing them as 'sad'.

Children today talk a lot about 'Respect' and everything that means. They expect respect of adults – of teachers, parents, marketers, the media, and of each other – actually they demand it. Sadly though, life can be fearful for children. Just think what they have learnt about in the last couple of years: terrorism, war, tsunami, hurricanes, global warming, and these events are coming into their homes every day through the media. The effect of all this is that children are beginning to take an interest in current affairs in a way they did not before. They want to help each other, they will discuss bullying in school, and they care about global warming and fair trade.

The iPod Generation

As a counter to the place technology plays in children's lives, there will be a re-emergence of quality family time. Technology can create a distance between children and their parents. We hear much about technology and the impact it has had on children's lives, and parents are aware that their children have a far higher exposure to technology than when they were young. A modern baby is born, and instead of a rattle to play with, is now given a plethora of toys that make noises, light up, demand interactivity. We know from studies in neuroscience that the human brain has mostly developed by 24 months. Infants and toddlers love bright clear images and music, especially repetitive tunes, and research shows that cognitive ability can be stimulated by sight and sound at this age. So in many ways technology can have a positive impact on young children.

We have all been impressed by the increased number of children reading, encouraged no doubt by J.K. Rowling and Jacqueline Wilson. But literacy level among children remains a concern. In Japan we have the phenomenon of e-books, that is reading full length novels on mobile phones (Japan has 85 million mobile phone owners). Leading this is Bandai Networks, with 60% of their subscribers teenagers and early 20s, and 70% of these are logging on daily to read their e-books, especially girls. For many trends in technology we need to look to Japan.

Technology though has the effect on children of allowing them to entertain themselves; they may be interacting with the technology, but not other people. The child watching their own TV in their multi-functional bedroom, going online on their own wireless broadband connection, and, even if they are talking to friends on MSN, much of this is done alone. But what are the social implications of this? Increasingly more mums are working (7 out of 10), a necessity

brought about by expensive housing and lifestyle. Time short but cash rich parents are increasingly becoming aware that time spent with family, the ubiquitous 'quality time', is important. Parents seek fun as much as children, and leisure activities that offer entertainment for both will excel.

The Jamie Oliver Effect

Through his TV series (Jamie's School Dinners), Jamie Oliver managed to persuade the Government to release £280 million to tackle the school meal crisis. We continually read the headlines: children's rates of obesity are getting higher, and this has been partly caused by children given junk food and fizzy drinks. Another cause is the lack of exercise that children have, in comparison to their parents when they were children. Figures show that while average weight has increased over the last 20 years, calorific intake has actually decreased. This is in part due to children having far more to entertain them at home – gaming, the internet, iPods etc. But as we know it also links to the fearful world we live in, concern about Stranger Danger and road safety, and parents not wishing their children to play outside, walk to school on their own, or play in parks unsupervised.

This means that there is a trend to encourage children to eat better and healthier, and to take more exercise, and this is happening across much of the world where childhood obesity is a problem. As a result, food manufacturers are responding by introducing ever more healthy food and drink products that not only taste good, but will also appeal to children's sense of fun and adventure. We are also seeing a trend towards organic food, locally produced food, and farmers' markets, all of which appeal to children, and such food is getting cheaper.

Another trend linked into this is ways to encourage children to 'get active', and take more exercise. Sport and activity is going to grow amongst all children, not just those that are naturally athletic. This will see new products being introduced that can be used in the home, and in small gardens. And activity will become a family activity, allowing busy working parents to spend quality time with their children, while having fun and getting fit.

Conclusion

In looking at trends we need to consider social change as well as marketing trends. The pre-teen market, or 'Pre-Whatever' Generation as I have described it, is increasingly becoming socially responsible; younger children are taking a keen interest in their world and what is happening to it, and they are expecting to be heard. Fair trade and ethical practice will be expected, and 'respect' will be paramount.

Technology can have a positive impact on children's lives, and help their development, but it may actually make them more isolated. The 'iPod Generation' is one with busy parents, and family fun will become increasingly important; spending quality time as a family creates many opportunities for marketers.

Changes to food and drink consumption brought about by increased concern about childhood obesity and 'The Jamie Oliver Effect' will see an increased demand for healthy food and drink, and a growth in locally produced and organic food. Families will begin to embrace healthy eating, and supermarkets and food manufacturers will be responding to this.

Brands that recognise these factors will be the success stories of the next decade.

www.kidsandyouth.com

Responsible Brands

By Dr Agnes Nairn, Senior Lecturer in Marketing, School of Management, University of Bath /EM-Lyon, France & Nick Davies, Managing Director WWAV Rapp Collins Bristol

Today's brands play a bigger part in children's lives than ever before.

Firstly, much more brand marketing is targeted directly at kids through TV, internet sites, SMS, magazines, celebrity endorsement and product placement. A lot of kids now spend much of their time in their own 'media bedsits' with not only a TV but video, DVD, games console and internet access. These are pretty much adult-free zones.

Secondly, kids have more disposable income to spend on brands. They spent £3 billion of their own money last year and influenced a further £3 billion of family purchases.

So, given this intense commercial interest in our children, how do we ensure that the brands targeting our kids are responsible brands? And what do we mean by a responsible brand anyway? Responsible to whom? Responsible for what?

These questions have yet to be widely debated in the UK, as the direct targeting of kids is really a very recent phenomenon and this is, after all, the very first Kids Superbrands book. But responsible branding is an important issue for parents, brand owners, society as a whole and, of course, for the children themselves. We hope that the release of this first Kids Superbrands book will serve as a forum to explore and advance responsible branding.

Children's Protection or Children's Rights?

Before the debate can really get underway we need to be clear that there are currently two prominent views on children's consumption. On the one hand is a view that it is the duty of adults who care for children to protect them from profit-motivated influence which they may not understand. Organisations such as the Campaign for Commercial Free Childhood (CCFC) provide a strong voice here. The argument usually advanced under this viewpoint is that children are less able than adults to understand persuasive intent and need a guiding hand. On the other hand is the assumption that children have rights as consumers to be heard, to be satisfied and even to participate in the creation of children's products and services. The recent innovative youth research conducted by the Tate in London which resulted in a massive increase in youth attendance and interest in the art gallery is an excellent example here.

So a responsible children's brand must fulfil two principle duties. First not to take advantage of a child's lack of experience when creating a marketing communications campaign and second to listen to its junior customers.

Let's take each of these duties in turn.

Not Taking Advantage of Kids' Lack of Experience

How experienced are our kids when it comes to deciding which marketing messages to accept and which to reject? The media presents us with two images of today's child: in-your-face, media-savvy and cynical on the one hand and innocent, vulnerable and exploited on the other. Parents know that neither of these stereotypes adequately describes every child. Our children are all different and the way they negotiate the media and the commercial messages sent to them depends on a complex combination of factors such as their age, parenting styles, peer pressure, socio economic background and personality. So neither zealous over-protection of children by banning them from watching commercial TV or using the internet, nor a completely laissez faire attitude of leaving kids to negotiate their own way through the world of advertising and marketing is particularly helpful. Instead parents, children and brand owners need to work together to ensure that all parties really do understand each other's intentions and that nothing is covert or manipulative.

So here are a few ideas for parents to consider and to discuss with their children.

Parents should be aware of some of the codes designed to protect them and their kids. Advertising on broadcast TV and press is carefully watched over by the Advertising Standards Association which ensures that what we see is 'legal, decent, honest and truthful'. And, yes, the 9 o'clock watershed still exists. But parents should also be aware that advertising regulation is not at all harmonised across the world. As more and more international channels become available on satellite and cable, and as kids can video late night programmes to watch whenever they want, there is a limit to what the authorities can do to ensure children watch suitable material. So chat to your kids about what they watch and look out for the following sorts of activities which a responsible brand should not be engaging in.

A responsible brand should not:

- make your child feel that they are inadequate in some way if they do not possess the brand
- present material which your child does not want to see (e.g. sexually explicit images)
- obtain information about your child without your permission (this is against the code of the Market Research Society)
- attempt to sell products under the guise of doing research
- try to drive a wedge between you and your children by implying that parents are 'uncool'
- explicitly recruit children to influence their peers

Treating Kids with Respect

The second duty of the responsible brand is to respect children as consumers. Research conducted by the National Consumer Council in 2005 showed that children often feel talked down to and ripped off. These findings are echoed by a study published by the University of Bath in 2006. A few quotes from children in the Bath study make the point well.

Kids don't respond well to adverts which seem to make promises that aren't delivered on when the product is bought. This is a comment about an action figure by an 11 year-old boy:

"I think I was interested in them coz when they advertised them they showed them really like, in places that suited them, but when you actually got them, you didn't actually get the setting … it was just your bedroom."

And here an eight year-old girl is talking about a playground game:

"We thought they were really good and then once we bought one we thought it was a bit rubbish."

Children are also aware of the concept of value for money:

"The price is £14.99 for a little piece of plastic with hair and a face." (10 year-old girl talking about a doll)

"They were very expensive. Well, not very expensive but it's an awful lot for just some bits of plastic and metal." (11 year-old boy talking about an action toy)

And they are often very cynical about marketing practice:

"…and they used to sell them at far too expensive cause they knew that everyone wanted to buy them so they were like £6 for one thing… so they made them extremely expensive cause they knew it'd go out of fashion soon so if they could quickly sell them now for lots of money then they would get loads." (11 year-old boy talking about an action toy)

These children's views serve as a warning to brands that they need to treat these increasingly valuable customers with respect. And they are probably heartening to parents too – they show that even young children increasingly understand the commercial world.

But toys are one thing. Where should we stand on the targeting of 13 year-olds with plastic of the card variety? Are the branded, pre-paid cash cards being targeted at our teenage kids as we write this simply 21st century pocket money, or are they encouraging an acceptance of credit at a dangerously early age? Clearly these pre-pay cards cannot offer a credit facility, but are advertisements in teenage magazines urging young readers to 'splash the cash' with these cards either wanted or warranted?

Companies and marketers have a huge responsibility to the kids – and indeed to the integrity of the brands they work for – to think carefully before they communicate with kids. Above all, of course, kids want to have fun, to be creative, to be healthy and to be happy.

The very best brands not only respect the boundaries, but they also actively help kids to do all these things. We are proud to be associated with Kids Superbrands and the recognition of responsible brands which are showing the way.

www.wwavrcbristol.co.uk

A lifelong addiction
By Kirsten Grant
Marketing Director
Puffin Books

'Daddy' she [Matilda] said, 'do you think you could buy me a book?'
'A book?' he said. What d'you want a flaming book for?'
'To read, Daddy.'
'What's wrong with the telly, for heaven's sake? We've got a lovely telly with a 12-inch screen and now you come asking for a book! You're getting spoiled, my girl!'
Matilda by Roald Dahl

How we **long** to hear children say these words. Watch them abandon their Playstations, iPods and mobiles in favour of a good book instead. This may seem like an impossible dream – but it's not. We **can** convince children that reading is enriching in so many ways, is capable of transporting them to worlds they don't know exist, learn that other children are going through similar things and find out what other people are

thinking, so that they can see the other side of the story. And, even more importantly, learn to treat their imagination like a playground – a wonderfully unrestricted place they can nip off to at any time for endless fun, dreaming and enjoyment. The crucial question is: how?

Australian children's author, Paul Jennings, says in 'The Reading Bug...and how to help your child catch it': 'The one person who will do more than anyone else to help your children learn to read … is you'. And you can do this in so many ways – lead by example – read **to** your child and **in front** of your child – there's no greater enticement, especially for boys, than to see their dad reading for pleasure – and it doesn't have to be just books – comics, newspapers, the back of the cereal packet, pages on the internet, football programmes, magazines – these are all equally valid means of reading. As adults don't live on a constant diet of Tolstoy and 'The South Bank Show', but snack on 'The Da Vinci Code' and 'Footballers' Wives', children, too, should be able to pick and choose what they want to read – the essential thing is to keep them reading.

While we are all well aware of the importance of books for educational and leisure purposes, it is rarely acknowledged that they are also a valuable source of security and comfort to children. Books and reading can provide an emotional crutch in many ways: firstly, as a sharing activity which enables them to spend quality time with their parent/carer; secondly, as a means by which they can

encounter subjects and situations outside of their own, limited personal experience; thirdly, as a confirmation of personal experience; fourthly, as a means of developing their sense of empathy; and finally, as a way of allaying their often unspoken doubts and fears about the world they live in.

Right from birth, the age-old tradition of the bedtime story is absolutely crucial. Children actually look forward to this time of the day, not only because it is an excuse to say awake longer, but also because it helps them wind down from a busy day, they get to hear their favourite stories, they get to spend special one-on-one time with their parents...the list is endless.

'This act of love forms an association between the child and books. The word 'book' brings pleasure. The feel, look and smell of books is forever linked to feelings of warmth, security and love. You have started a lifelong love affair between a child and reading.'
Paul Jennings

So, no matter how many things you have on your 'to do' list every evening, if you can hear the strain of the opening bars of the Eastenders' theme tune or, even if you're just feeling plain shattered after a busy day, **try** to make even the shortest amount of time to cuddle up together in bed to enjoy a story, thinking that you're both going to come out winners at the end of the day – because, believe it or not, storytelling is also a brilliant way of getting children off to sleep!

Choice of reading matter, too, is incredibly important. Faced with over 10,000 new children's books being published every year, knowing what to buy can be a minefield, and an extremely daunting prospect. Get into the habit of visiting the library and the local bookshop as a family activity, and just spend time browsing. There has never been a better time to buy/borrow children's books. The shelves are literally bursting with brilliant books for all ages that look utterly irresistible with gorgeous packaging, enticing covers and pages that are simply oozing with page-turning storylines that your children won't be able to put down. Pick the brains of your local librarian/children's bookseller and start with classics by big name authors; The Very Hungry Caterpillar by Eric Carle, the Hairy Maclary stories by Lynley Dodd and Peepo! and Each Peach Pear Plum by Janet & Allan Ahlberg for babies and toddlers, Mr Majeika by Humphrey Carpenter, The Witch's Dog by Frank Rodgers and The Worst Witch series for developing readers and Jacqueline Wilson, J.K. Rowling, Artemis Fowl and Roald Dahl for older readers. You could even introduce some books **you** enjoyed as a child and, as you gain in confidence and find the kinds of stories your child likes to read, you can cast your net wider and expose them to the wealth of stories, poetry and non-fiction available (many on audio, too). Their reading diet needs to be as varied and balanced as the one that they eat (even if it is Turkey Twizzlers from time to time) and wouldn't it be fantastic to see them devour it in exactly the same way?

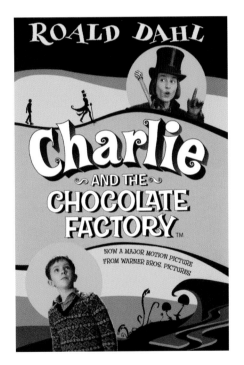

Looking out for the latest TV and cinema blockbusters can be an opportunistic way of using media hype to introduce your children to some fantastic stories too, many of which have originally come from books, such as The Chronicles of Narnia, The Lord of the Rings, the Harry Potter stories and Charlie and the Chocolate Factory, Tracy Beaker and the fabulous new Charlie and Lola series on CBeebies. If they enjoyed the film and TV programmes, then they're bound to enjoy the book, discovering a whole wealth of adventures by the same author into the bargain.

The 'crossover' genre has also become extremely popular recently – books which can be enjoyed by both children and adults, such as How I Live Now by Meg Rosoff, The Curious Incident of the Dog in the Night-Time by Mark Haddon and the bestselling new Young Bond series by Charlie Higson. And who knows, maybe you'll have to race your children to the bookshelf…

www.puffin.co.uk

Kids Charities

Here you will find an overview of some of the leading children's charities whose work aids the health, safety and happiness of children throughout the UK.

Action for Sick Children

www.actionforsickchildren.org
Tel: 01455 845 600
Registered charity no: 296295

"Action for Sick Children's mission is to ensure that healthcare in the UK meets the unique needs of all children and young people and their families.

With over 40 years' experience, Action for Sick Children campaigns on all aspects of healthcare, whether in hospital or at home and from national policies to individual family cases. We believe that family-focused environments, in addition to excellent medical services, are important to aiding recovery.

We help all families who require support irrespective of the difficulties involved. Every year millions of children receive treatment in GP surgeries and hospitals all over the UK, with over three million attending hospitals for accident and emergency treatment.

Children can be extremely vulnerable, both physically and emotionally and need special care and attention when they are sick and injured. We aim to ensure that sick children's special needs are taken into account and the whole child is treated – not just the illness or injury."

British Association for Adoption & Fostering (BAAF)

www.baaf.org.uk
Tel: 020 7421 2600
Registered charity no: 275689

"The British Association for Adoption & Fostering (BAAF) has been working for the past 25 years to find new permanent families for children, and to ensure that children in foster care receive the best possible support.

They achieve this through a variety of ways, such as 'Family Finding'. Through a monthly newspaper, Be My Parent, they find families for around 300 children a year – children who often wait for a long time to be placed, like older children, groups of brothers and sisters, disabled children and children from black and ethnic minority backgrounds.

The BAAF also offers telephone advice, information leaflets and booklets to over 10,000 adoptive parents, foster carers, children, adopted adults and social workers each year, covering all issues relating to adoption and fostering.

The BAAF campaigns nationally and locally, for changes to policy and practice to improve the lives of children in care and in 2003 won an IPR Award for Excellence for public affairs."

CHILDREN 1ST

www.children1st.org.uk
Helpline: 0808 800 222
Registered charity no: SC 016092

"CHILDREN 1ST, the working name of the Royal Scottish Society for Prevention of Cruelty to Children, is one of Scotland's leading child welfare charities.

For more than 120 years it has been working to give every child in Scotland a safe and secure childhood. We support families under stress, protect children from harm and neglect, help them to recover from abuse and promote children's rights and interests.

A key part of our work in helping children is by aiding their parents. Our free helpline, ParentLine Scotland, supports parents so that they can provide the best possible care for their children.

Keeping children safe is everyone's business. Help us give children and young people who need us a brighter future."

BBC Children in Need

www.bbc.co.uk/pudsey
Tel: 020 8576 7788
Registered charity no: 802052

"BBC Children in Need helps disadvantaged children and young people in the UK.

Some have experienced domestic violence, neglect, homelessness or sexual abuse, and others have suffered from chronic illness, or have had to learn to deal with profound disabilities from a very young age.

Many organisations supported by the charity aim to create a lasting impact on children's lives. Some offer low achieving children from areas of deprivation a chance to develop their educational skills and ambitions and others create opportunities for young people who are homeless or socially excluded, to enable them to move forward and secure a fulfilling future.

The charity offers grants to voluntary groups, community groups and registered charities around the UK that focus on improving children's lives. Grants are targeted on the areas of greatest need and money is allocated geographically to ensure that children in all corners of the UK receive a fair share of what is raised."

ChildLine

www.childline.org.uk
Helpline: 0800 1111
Registered charity no: 1003758

"ChildLine is the UK's free telephone helpline for children and young people. Trained volunteer counsellors are available 24 hours a day, every day, to offer children support, advice and protection.

Since ChildLine was launched, in 1986, it has helped more than 1.8 million children and young people, who turn to it for help with problems like bullying, family tensions, physical or sexual abuse and concerns about friends and family members.

Children trust ChildLine. Counsellors can help a child to identify an adult in their life who they might feel able to talk to, and give the child support and encouragement to do that. When necessary ChildLine acts in partnership with the police, social services or the ambulance service to ensure a child's safety.

ChildLine doesn't just listen to children - it gives them a voice. It raises awareness among the public and decision-makers and also works with schools to run anti-bullying peer support schemes.

ChildLine and the NSPCC joined together on February 1st 2006."

Children's Heart Federation

www.childrens-heart-fed.org.uk
Helpline: 0808 808 5000
Registered charity no: 800525

"The Children's Heart Federation is the umbrella body for voluntary organisations working to meet the needs of children and young people with congenital heart conditions and their families.

We aim to improve the quality of life of people living with congenital or childhood acquired heart disease by providing information, working to gain recognition of their needs and by ensuring adequate resources are available to meet these needs.

We support families with 'heart children' by giving information and advice, providing contact details for CHF member groups, giving grants to parents for equipment and support and organising meetings and family get-togethers.

We work together with CHF member groups to achieve our aims and support them in developing strong voices and effective services.

We also work with professional partners to ensure improvements in health and social and educational provision for children with heart conditions."

CLIC Sargent

www.clicsargent.org.uk
Tel: 0845 301 0031
Helpline: 0800 197 0068
Registered charity no: 802396

"CLIC Sargent is the UK's leading children's cancer charity – caring from birth, through adolescence to adulthood. Formerly CLIC and Sargent Cancer Care for Children, we have combined our strengths by merging in January 2005. We want to see a world where all children and young people with cancer live life to the full. Our promise is to be there for each family every step of the way, providing individual support to children and young people with cancer and leukemia and their families.

Every 48 hours, 10 children or young people are diagnosed with cancer or leukemia. CLIC Sargent offers a lifeline to those children and their families by providing services tailored to their needs. We give children, young people and their families a strong national voice, helping them to be heard and understood and are committed to improving survival rates further by helping to fund research into causes and treatments."

Contact a Family

www.cafamily.org.uk
Helpline: 0808 808 3555
Registered charity no: 284912

"Contact a Family provides advice, information and support to families with disabled children across the UK, whatever the child's disability or condition.

The charity's national freephone helpline provides advice on all aspects of raising a disabled child, including claiming benefits and tax credits, childcare and education, leisure opportunities and transition to adulthood.

The helpline also draws on the Contact a Family Directory of Specific Conditions and Rare Disorders to provide medical information and details of parents' support groups. Where there is no support group the charity will link families on a one-to-one basis, via the helpline or its dedicated website, www.makingcontact.org.

The charity also has a network of national, regional and project offices which provide specialist local knowledge, run workshops and social events, and in some areas, work with families individually. Contact a Family increasingly works with parents' groups to shape local services and campaigns nationally to improve the lives of families with disabled children."

Great Ormond Street Hospital Children's Charity (GOSHCC)

www.gosh.org
Tel: 020 7916 5678
Registered charity no: 235825

"For over 150 years Great Ormond Street Hospital (GOSH) has been treating sick children and pushing forward the boundaries of child health as one of the best paediatric hospitals in the world. Every year 100,000 desperately ill children are referred to GOSH from hospitals throughout the UK in order to benefit from its world-class expertise and specialised care.

However, much of the hospital's buildings and facilities are very outdated and there is an urgent need to redevelop the site. Great Ormond Street Hospital Children's Charity (GOSHCC) needs to raise £150 million in the next five years to complete the first phase of this vital project and we are reliant on public generosity to achieve this. We need to bring the hospital's facilities up to 21st century standards, to provide care in a more comfortable and convenient way, reduce unnecessary stays in hospital and provide better facilities for the 1,000 parents a week who need to sleep near to their child."

Comic Relief

www.comicrelief.com
Tel: 020 7820 5555
Registered charity no: 326568

"Comic Relief was launched from the Safawa refugee camp in Sudan, on Christmas Day 1985, in response to crippling famine in Africa. The aim was to take a fresh and fun approach to fundraising and, through events like Red Nose Day, inspire those who hadn't previously been interested in charity, to get involved. Since then there have been 10 Red Nose Days and two Sport Reliefs, raising over £400 million. Red Nose Day 2005 raised over £65 million.

Comic Relief has worked with some of the biggest names in entertainment, sport and business and tackles some of the biggest issues facing people across the world. Their work ranges from supporting projects that help children who are living rough in India to community programmes helping the elderly across the UK. A number of high profile partnerships have brought in millions of pounds to help reach these aims but the biggest group of supporters remains schools with over 60% taking part in Red Nose Day 2005."

Global Angels

www.globalangels.org
Tel: 0870 765 2643
Registered charity no: 1102926

"Global Angels is an innovative international children's charity promoting the causes of children around the world. We have an ambitious vision to inspire millions of people from all walks of life and spheres of influence to put their compassion into action and become 'Angels'.

We will be hosting an on-going series of high profile creative Global Angels concerts, events and television programmes. Funds raised will support established, long-term development projects that are making a significant impact on the lives of children. Projects are being selected from the UK and every country across the globe.

Global Angels promises that for every pound that we will receive, that pound will go directly to support projects helping children at a grass-root level."

Home-Start

www.home-start.org.uk
Freephone: 0800 068 63 68
Registered charity no: 1108837

"Home-Start is a 32 year-old national charity that recruits and trains volunteers to befriend and support families with children under five, by visiting them in their own homes.

The charity offers friendship and informal support to parents with young children, in local communities throughout the UK, so that every child can have a good start in life. Volunteers visit for a couple of hours each week and help families for as long as is necessary – ranging sometimes from months to years – in varied situations such as isolation, physical or mental illness, bereavement, multiple births, or simply finding parenthood difficult to cope with.

Home-Start currently has 11,000 home-visiting volunteers supporting 31,000 families and 68,000 children through 337 local schemes. In some of our schemes volunteers run family groups, specialist support groups, day trips and parties – additional services provided outside of our core work, that of visiting families in their homes."

Kids Company

www.kidsco.org.uk
Tel: 0845 644 6838
Registered charity no: 1068298
"Kids Company was founded in 1996 to meet the needs of exceptionally vulnerable young people.

The organisation values the emotional relationship between the caring adult and the child. Young people can refer either themselves or their friends. Many have been exposed to relentless violence, sexual and physical abuse and are devastated by loneliness.

The child is seen as the primary client to whom Kids Company is accountable. Kids Company makes available the services of social workers, psychotherapists and caring adults to some 5,000 children in inner city schools each year. A further 600 children access Kids Company's children's centre, which provides education and a holistic, therapeutic and practical intervention.

Independent evaluations have commended Kids Company, recognising it for providing exceptional service provision. Children give Kids Company 100% impact rating and 95% satisfaction rating (Source: NCB Evaluation 2002). Kids Company's ultimate aim is to restore a safe childhood to children."

National Deaf Children's Society

www.ndcs.org.uk
Helpline: 0808 800 8880
Registered charity no: 1016532
"The National Deaf Children's Society (NDCS) is the only UK charity solely dedicated to supporting deaf children and young people, their families and the professionals working with them.

Three babies are born deaf every day, 90% to hearing parents with little or no experience of deafness. Deafness makes it harder to learn to communicate and many families face challenges establishing good communication with their deaf child.

The NDCS vision is of a future without barriers for every deaf child. We offer clear, balanced information and support to families through our NDCS freephone helpline, a network of family officers and volunteers, and family events. Staff can advise on education and financial issues, offering advocacy where needed. The NDCS also organises a range of sports and activity events for young deaf people, helping them to develop social skills, confidence and independence."

NSPCC

www.nspcc.org.uk
Helpline: 0808 800 5000
Registered charity no: 216401
"The National Society for the Prevention of Cruelty to Children (NSPCC) is the UK's leading charity specialising in child protection and the prevention of cruelty to children.

The society has been protecting children from cruelty since 1884, when it was founded by Benjamin Waugh. It is the only children's charity with statutory powers enabling it to act to safeguard children at risk. It has 177 teams and projects around the UK as well as five Divisional Offices, a National Centre (Weston House) in London and the NSPCC Training and Consultancy Centre in Leicester.

The NSPCC provides an independent campaigning voice for children. It works to influence government on legislation and policy that affect the lives of children and families, and runs public education campaigns to raise awareness of, and encourage action to prevent, child abuse.

ChildLine and the NSPCC joined together on February 1st 2006."

Mencap

www.askmencap.info
Helpline: 0808 808 1111
Registered charity no: 222377
"Mencap is the UK's leading learning disability charity working with children and adults with a learning disability, their families and carers.

Together, we fight for equal rights, campaign for greater opportunities and challenge attitudes and prejudice. We provide advice and support to meet people's needs throughout their lives.

A learning disability does not stop someone from learning and achieving a lot in life, if they get the right support. Mencap helps people with a learning disability to live their lives in ways that they choose. There are 1.5 million people in the UK with a learning disability.

Mencap runs three national colleges for young people with a learning disability, where they learn essential life skills. We also provide some support services and develop innovative projects, that involve and engage with children and young people with a learning disability."

NCH

www.nch.org.uk
Tel: 020 7704 7000
Registered charity no: 4764232
"NCH is the leading UK provider of; family and community centres, children's services in rural areas, services for disabled children and their families and services for young people leaving care.

NCH runs more than 500 projects, supporting over 140,000 of the UK's most vulnerable and excluded children, young people and families, many of whom face difficulties such as poverty, disability and abuse.

We believe that all children and young people have unique potential and that they should have the support and opportunities they need to reach it. We have been working to make this vision a reality for over 135 years."

Rainbow Trust Children's Charity

www.rainbowtrust.org.uk
Tel: 01372 363438
Registered charity no: 1070532
"Rainbow Trust Children's Charity, established in 1986, provides practical and emotional support to families when a child has a life threatening or terminal illness.

Rainbow Trust has two respite houses, Rainbow House in Surrey and Rainbow Fernstone in Northumberland, where families can spend time together in a relaxing, supportive environment.

Rainbow Trust also supports families in their own homes through a team of Family Support Workers. These workers give practical and emotional help and will respond to the needs of individual family members. This service provides a 24-hour flexible response to crisis, i.e. if a child needs to be hospitalised and there is no one to care for the other children.

Families who have a child or young person up to the age of 18 years with a life threatening or terminal condition are eligible for our services from diagnosis, through to treatment and beyond."

Round Table Children's Wish

www.rtcw.org
Tel: 01202 514 515
Registered charity no: 3298944

"Round Table Children's Wish is a registered charity that grants wishes to children throughout Great Britain and Ireland who are aged 18 and under and are suffering from life-threatening illnesses. Founded in 1990 the charity has now granted over 950 wishes. The aim is to fulfil a child's secret dream. This may be to meet their heroes and idols from the worlds of sport, television or popular music, or perhaps to give them the opportunity to swim with dolphins or meet their favourite cartoon characters. For others, a quiet holiday with family members or the gift of a computer or playhouse may be their ideal wish.

Even in the closest of families children have a secret dream that they do not share with anyone else. In each case we ensure that the wish we grant is truly that of the child, not what someone else assumes they might like!"

Shelter

www.shelter.org.uk
Helpline: 0808 800 4444
Registered charity no: 263710

"Bad housing wrecks lives. We are the fifth richest country in the world, and yet more than one million children in Britain wake up every day in housing that is run-down, overcrowded or dangerous. Many have even lost their home altogether and are forced to wait in emergency accommodation for a permanent home; sometimes this can take years. Bad housing is making our children ill, robbing them of a decent education and damaging their future.

Shelter believes everyone should have a home. We help 100,000 people a year fight for their rights, get back on their feet, and find and keep a home. We also tackle the root causes of Britain's housing crisis by campaigning for new laws, policies and solutions."

The Children's Society

www.childrenssociety.org.uk
Supporter Action Line: 0845 300 1128
Registered charity no: 221124

"Children at risk on the streets, children in trouble with the law, young refugees, disabled children: these are the priority groups that The Children's Society helps the most.

We operate around 60 projects across England, employing over 500 specialist staff. We provide guidance to young runaways when they find home has become unbearable. We make sure that children in the justice system are treated like children, not locked away as adult criminals. We help refugee children – who have often suffered enough before they reach this country – find the accommodation and education that they deserve. And we communicate with disabled children in order to understand their real needs. Every year we work with 50,000 children directly, while our research and campaigning helps thousands more.

The Children's Society was founded 125 years ago. While our work is based on Christian principles, the children we work with and those who support us, come from any faith, or none at all."

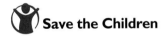

Save the Children

www.savethechildren.org.uk
Tel: 020 7012 6400
Registered charity no: 213890

"Save the Children works in the UK and across the World. Emergency relief runs alongside long-term development and prevention work to help children, their families and communities to be self-sufficient. We learn from the reality of children's lives and campaign for solutions to the problems they face. We gain expertise through our projects around the world and use that knowledge to educate and advise others.

All our work is underpinned by our commitment to making a reality of the rights of children, first spelled out by our founders and now enshrined in the United Nation's Convention on the Rights of the Child. All children deserve the best start in life and have the right to live in a world where they have hope and opportunity. Children need special care and assistance, without which they cannot fully develop their potential."

SPARKS

www.sparks.org.uk
Tel: 020 7799 2111
Registered charity no: 1003825

"SPARKS funds pioneering medical research that has a practical, positive impact on the lives of babies and children.

Since 1991, SPARKS has funded over 160 medical projects in the UK, committing over £12 million to tackle conditions as diverse as cerebral palsy, meningitis, the dangers of premature birth, spina bifida, childhood arthritis and cancers.

In the UK, many important areas of paediatric research depend heavily on funding from charities like SPARKS rather than the public purse. It's this knowledge that motivates the dedicated SPARKS team."

The Prince's Trust

www.princes-trust.org.uk
Tel: 0800 842 842
Registered charity no: 1079675

"Youth charity The Prince's Trust helps change young lives in the UK. It gives practical and financial support, developing skills such as confidence and motivation. It works with 14-30 year-olds who have struggled at school, have been in care, are long-term unemployed or have been in trouble with the law. In 30 years The Prince of Wales' charity has helped over half a million young people and continues to support 100 more every day.

All of our activities – programmes, partnerships, fundraising – have one overall purpose: to reach young people in the UK who face more barriers than most and to help them get past those barriers so they can get their lives working and make a positive contribution to society. The Prince's Trust supports young people in a number of ways, including cash awards, business start-up support, leaving care initiatives and overseas community projects."

The Shooting Star Children's Hospice

www.shootingstar.org.uk
Tel: 020 8481 8180
Registered charity no: 1047916
"Shooting Star House, Children's Hospice provides holistic care to children and young people with life-limiting conditions, and provides support to the whole family through a range of professional care services, both at the hospice and in the comfort of the families' own home. Respite Care, Hospice at Home Care and specialist End of Life Care are available to our families free of charge, 365 days a year.

Facilities at the hospice include 10 children's bedrooms, two of which are en-suite, a hydrotherapy pool and spa, multi-sensory room and music therapy room, along with play areas and six family rooms and a family lounge.

As the charity receives no statutory government funding, the £2.5 million needed each and every year has to come from voluntary donations and fundraising. To this end, we hope that we can continue to rely on generous public support."

The Variety Club Children's Charity

www.varietyclub.org.uk
Tel: 020 7428 8134
Registered charity no: 209259
"The Variety Club Children's Charity improves the lives of sick, disabled and disadvantaged children across the UK.

Our work can range from funding major hospital appeals to providing basic items that will improve the lives of individual children. Each year we donate a variety of items, including specialist beds, car seats, sensory equipment, wheelchairs and standing frames.

We benefit from the hard work of several hundred members whose voluntary contributions mean that at least 90p in every £1 raised goes directly to the children who need it."

UNICEF

www.unicef.org.uk
Tel: 0870 606 3377
Registered charity no: 1072612
"For 60 years UNICEF has been the world's leader for children, working on the ground in 155 countries and territories to help children survive and thrive, from early childhood through to adolescence.

As the world's largest provider of vaccines for poor countries, UNICEF supports child health and nutrition, good water and sanitation, quality basic education for all boys and girls and the protection of children from violence, exploitation and AIDS. UNICEF is funded entirely by the voluntary contributions donated by individuals, businesses, foundations and governments."

The Together Trust

www.togethertrust.org.uk
Tel: 0161 283 4848
Registered charity no: 209782
"The Together Trust is a charity, operating since 1870 in the North of England and North Wales, that provides care, education, support and improved life opportunities for young people in need.

We serve children and young people who are experiencing emotional, behavioural or social difficulties, physical and/or learning disabilities and autistic spectrum disorders. Our services cover residential homes, fostering, adoption, community services, special schools and a college.

The young people we support often experience an additional disadvantage from their social exclusion and the fact that they do not fit easily into society's mainstream provision. The Trust is committed to increasing life opportunities for young people in need, with a focus on care, education and support.

As a registered charity The Together Trust requires partners, particularly from the business sector, to raise awareness of its work and provide support that will help maintain, develop and create services in the region and beyond."

Tommy's, the baby charity

www.tommys.org
Tel: 08707 707070
Pregnancy information line: 0870 7773060
Registered charity no: 1060508
"We are committed to funding medical research and providing information to help more mums and dads through a healthy pregnancy and birth.

In the UK, a baby is lost every two minutes as a result of miscarriage, stillbirth or premature birth. Tommy's is the only UK charity solely dedicated to maximising health in pregnancy. We are already bringing more babies safely into the world by funding pioneering medical research into the causes of pregnancy complications and providing pregnancy information. But still a quarter of all families are affected by the loss of a baby each year.

It is only with continued support that we can do more to prevent complications in pregnancy and give every baby the best chance for the best start in life."

WellChild

www.wellchild.org.uk
Helpline: 0845 458 8171
Registered charity no: 289600
"More than 750,000 children in the UK suffer from severe long-standing illness and disability. Their illness impacts on every member of the family, which is often stretched to breaking point. WellChild cares for the individual needs of sick children and their families whatever the cause, through practical support and research into new treatment and cures."

Whizz-Kidz

Whizz-Kidz
move a life forward

Whizz-Kidz
www.whizz-kidz.org.uk
Tel: 020 7233 6600
Registered charity no: 802872

"Whizz-Kidz aim to ensure that every physically disabled child fulfils their potential and leads an active childhood. Like all children, disabled children need to move around independently and enjoy the freedom to live full and active lives with their families and friends.

The NHS is often unable to provide the mobility equipment, training and advice that they need. Looking after a disabled child can increase the emotional and physical strain on families. Having to spend time and effort in obtaining mobility equipment and support services is an additional stress.

This is where Whizz-Kidz comes in, changing disabled children's lives – literally overnight – by providing them with customised mobility equipment, training and advice.

But we also give them something much more important: the independence to live a life of freedom at home, at school and at play, the independence to be themselves."

Directory

adams kids
Adams Childrenswear Ltd
Attleborough House
Townsend Drive
Nuneaton
Warwickshire
CV11 6RU

Bambino Mio
Bambino Mio Ltd
12 Staveley Way
Brixworth
Northampton
NN6 9EU

Bounty
Bounty (UK) Ltd
Bounty House
Vinces Road
Diss
Norfolk
IP98 6BB

Britax
Britax Excelsior Ltd
1 Churchill Way West
Andover
Hampshire
SP10 3UW

British Airways London Eye
British Airways London Eye
Riverside Building
County Hall
Westminster Bridge Road
London
SE1 7PB

Caboodle Bags
Caboodle Bags
20 Priory Road
Faversham
Kent
ME13 7EJ

CASIO®
Casio Electronics Co. Ltd
Unit 6
1000 North Circular Road
London
NW2 7JD

Early Learning Centre
Early Learning Centre
Burdett House
15-16 Buckingham Street
London
WC2N 6DU

Eurocamp
Eurocamp
Hartford Manor
Greenbank Lane
Northwich
Cheshire
CW8 1HW

GEOMAG
Geomag SA
Palazzo Mercurio
Piazza Col.C. Bernasconi 5
6830 Chiasso
Switzerland

GRACO
Graco UK & Ireland
900 Pavilion Drive
Northampton Business Park
Northampton
NN4 7RG

Great Little Trading Co.
GLTC Ltd
Jessica House
Red Lion Square
191 Wandsworth High Street
London
SW18 4LS

grobag®
gro-group™ International Ltd
Unit C4
Linhay Business Park
Ashburton
Devon
TQ13 7UP

Haliborange
Seven Seas Ltd
Hedon Road
Marfleet
Hull
HU9 5NJ

HARIBO®
Dunhills (Pontefract) plc
26 Front Street
Pontefract
West Yorkshire
WF8 1NJ

Heinz Spaghetti
H.J. Heinz Co. Ltd
Hayes
Middlesex
UB4 8AL

Junior
Future Publishing Ltd
2 Balcombe Street
London
NW1 6NW

Kellogg's Coco Pops
Kellogg Marketing and Sales
Company (UK) Ltd
The Kellogg Building
Talbot Road
Manchester
M16 0PU

Little Tikes
Little Tikes
900 Pavilion Drive
Northampton Business Park
Brackmills
Northampton
NN4 7RG

Matey
Sara Lee Household & Body Care
225 Bath Road
Slough
SL1 4AU

Milkshake!
Five
22 Long Acre
London
WC2E 9LY

Mother & Baby
Emap plc
Greater London House
Hampstead Road
London
NW1 7EJ

Mountain Buggy®
Mountain Buggy (UK) Ltd
Mill Farm Fairmile
Ottery St Mary
Devon
EX11 1LS

Müller®
Müller Dairy (UK) Ltd
Shrewsbury Road
Market Drayton
Shropshire
TF9 3SQ

MUNCH BUNCH
Nestlé UK Ltd
Chilled Dairy
St Georges House
Park Lane
Croydon
CR9 1NR

NIVEA Sun
Beiersdorf UK Ltd
2010 Solihull Parkway
Birmingham Business Park
Birmingham
B87 7YS

PEZ®
Dunhills (Pontefract) plc
26 Front Street
Pontefract
West Yorkshire
WF8 1NJ

Philips
Philips Domestic and Personal Appliances
Philips Centre
Guildford Business Park
Guildford
Surrey
GU2 8XH

Pizza Hut
Pizza Hut Ltd
1 Imperial Place
Elstree Way
Borehamwood
Herts
WD6 1JN

Practical Parenting
IPC SouthBank Publishing Company Ltd
King's Reach Tower
Stamford Street
London
SE1 9LS

Pregnancy & birth
Emap plc
Greater London House
Hampstead Road
London
NW1 7EJ

Sainsbury's Kids
J Sainsbury's plc
33 Holborn
London
EC1N 2HT

Silver Cross
Silver Cross UK Ltd
Nesfield House
Broughton Hall
Skipton
North Yorkshire
BD23 3AN

SMA
SMA Nutrition
Wyeth UK
Huntercombe Lane South
Taplow
Maidenhead
Berkshire
SL6 0PH

Speedo
Speedo UK
Ascot Road
Nottingham
NG8 5AJ

Sun-Pat
Premier Foods
Premier House
Centrium Business Park
Griffiths Way
St Albans
Hertfordshire
AL1 2RE

Sylvanian Families
Flair Leisure Products plc
Anne Boleyn House
Ewell Road
Cheam
Surrey
SM3 8BZ

The Children's Mutual
The Children's Mutual
BrockBourne House
77 Mount Ephraim
Tunbridge Wells
Kent
TN1 8GN

Tixylix®
Novartis Consumer Health Ltd
Wimblehurst Road
Horsham
West Sussex
RH12 5AB

Tommee Tippee
Jackel International Ltd
Northumberland Business Park West
Cramlington
Northumberland
NE23 7RH

Tumble Tots
Tumble Tots (UK) Ltd
Blue Bird Park
Bromsgrove Road
Halesowen
West Midlands
B62 0TT

Venture
Venture UK Ltd
Premier Park
Road One
Winsford
Cheshire
CW7 3PH

VERTBAUDET
Vertbaudet (UK) Ltd
Redcats
18 Canal Road
Bradford
West Yorkshire
BD99 4XB

VTech
VTech Electronics Europe plc
Napier Court
Abingdon Science Park
Abingdon
Oxfordshire
OX14 3YT